Owning My S.H.I.T!

Suffering Hardship Internalizing Trauma

Jolanda "Jo" Jones

Dedication

To my mom, Gwendolyn Jones-Harris, you inspire me, and I love you even though the truth of us is difficult.

To my grandmother, Claudina Jones, I am literally still alive because of your love and belief in me.

To my son, Jiovanni Jones, you are the best and greatest gift God ever gave me. You are, and always will be, my greatest accomplishment. It is because of my love for you that I had the courage to choose life over certain death.

To my dad, John Jones, the ghost of you shaped so much of me. I wish I could remember you. Until we meet again.

Acknowledgements

Mr. Dick Enberg, who first put a serious thought in my mind that I had a story to tell and suggesting then promising to write the foreword. I apologize for not finishing it before you died. Just know that your death kicked my tail into high gear to complete this.

Ms. Cherrise Traylor, for teaching me how to love, loving me and allowing me to be my misunderstood self without judgment. Your patience is remarkable and contagious, which is huge for me.

Mrs. Hazel West, maternal grandmother
Mr. Eugene West, maternal grandfather
Mr. Willie Jones, paternal grandfather
Aunt Cathy Jones Lewis, paternal aunt
Aunt Christal Jones Mercier, paternal aunt
Aunt Timothy McDade, paternal aunt
Mr. Deloyd Parker, activist mentor
Mr. Ester King, activist mentor
President Dr. Marguerite Ross Barnett, University of Houston, mentor
Professor Lawrence Curry, University of Houston
Professor Gene Smith, University of Houston
Professor Paul Janicke, University of Houston
Graduate Advisor Soror Diana Merritte, Alpha Kappa Alpha Sorority, Inc.
Line Sister Soror Lizanne Lavergne, Alpha Kappa Alpha Sorority, Inc.
Line Sister Soror Charlene Johnson, Alpha Kappa Alpha Sorority, Inc.

Line Sister Soror Cheryl Glover, Alpha Kappa Alpha
Sorority, Inc.
Mr. Keith Wade, political advisor
Mr. Grant Martin, political advisor
Coach Bridget North, Houston ISD.
Coach Barbara Papke, Alief ISD
Coach Marti L. Burch, Alief ISD
Coach Leonard Fawcett, Alief ISD
Coach Dorothy Dolittle, University of Houston
Coach Tom Tellez, University of Houston
Congressman/Lawyer Craig Washington, mentor
Mr. Roy Malonson, journalist
Ms. Michelle Mackey, lifelong friend
Ms. Kim Lawson, friend
President James Douglas, Texas Southern University, mentor
Ms. Laurie Boydstun Kane, high school teammate
Ms. Stacey Lackey, high school teammate
Ms. Kara Kellogg, middle school teammate
Superintendent Dr. Grenita Lathan, Houston ISD

Endorsements

I first met Jolanda in 1980 when we were in high school and on the varsity track team. I saw Jo walking to school one morning around dawn before track practice and asked her if she wanted a ride. Jo and I were team mates and I picked her up for practice every day. Though she was hesitant about sharing too much, I learned things about Jolanda and some of the S.H.I.T! that she constantly dealt with during our daily car rides. Even though we came from very different backgrounds, we developed a sincere and lasting friendship that has continued for almost forty years. I love how Jo's adverse circumstances never stopped her from becoming an honor student and elite athlete. In fact, her trials and tribulations only made her stronger and more determined to break the cycle. In her book, "Owning My S.H.I.T!", Jolanda shares with us a courageous and honest account of her constant challenges while growing up in Houston, Texas. Jo's journey from heartache and poverty to successful lawyer and champion for justice is truly awe-inspiring. The strength and emotion of "Owning My S.H.I.T!" will uplift all who read it. I am so proud of my friend, Jolanda Jones.

~Laurie B. Kane
Friends Over 40 Years
Plano, Texas

My first encounter with Jolanda Jones was at the University of Houston. I happened to stumble upon a protest on campus. She was protesting a vice presidential candidate, Dan Quayle, as a member of the Mexican American Students Organization. I was in awe because she was the only African American protesting with the group. She noticed I was empty handed and gave me a poster to hold up. Shortly thereafter, we became friends. During the time of our friendship, I observed a woman of strength both on and off the track. Jolanda was sassy, confident and brutally honest. She could walk into a room and effortlessly capture the attention of everyone. However, Jolanda suffered from internal struggles that she masked from most everyone. On the outside, she appeared to have it all. But internally, she struggled with self-esteem that would eventually lead her into an abusive relationship. I witnessed her S.H.I.T first hand. Her boyfriend was excessively possessive and completely controlled her. She often went against her grain while she was with him. Behind closed doors, he would make her perform sexual acts that she wasn't comfortable with but did it anyway. I witnessed his aggression one evening while we were at Yucatán Liquor Stand. He hit her in front of everyone. It hurt to see her broken. I tried to advise her to leave him, but she would not listen. I told her he wasn't going to change. This was the strong woman that I met defending and protesting something she strongly believed in. This was the woman who called you out if she felt you were wrong. This was the woman that would not go down without a fight. She was always two steps ahead of you. Sadly, she didn't see the beauty in herself and she struggled with it. Even though she could date anyone she wanted and had many men interested in her, she didn't think she was beautiful enough. She didn't see the beauty she had within. Because of it, she allowed this relationship to continue. However, Jolanda always finds a way to win. She is the epitome of survival of the fittest. She is relentless and has an unyielding gift of perseverance. Although she was faced with more than her fair share of hardships, she sits at the top of the mountain and is well equipped to pick herself up should she fall.

~**Rosemary Gomez Guerra**
College Friend of Jolanda Jones
Mission, Texas

Jolanda Felicia Jones - a name that evokes pride, love, protection, strength, lore, and confusion. My sister has been more than a role model. She has consistently been my biggest cheerleader/advocate and protector. For many years, I did not understand why she was protective to the point of irritation. I am now aware of her obsession with protecting me. She has protected me my entire life. She protected me from my mother, my uncle, my coach, even male friends, and anyone with intentions to hurt me sexually, psychologically, or physically. Jolanda made sure my experiences were better than hers. Our respective approaches to life are quite different and a result of our collective childhood experiences. I was protected. She was not. Even though I was abused, it was not to that degree. She has had to endure unspeakable abuse as a child and as an adult. Thus, it has taken my sister years to truly have joy and happiness in her life. Despite the negativity, Jolanda has succeeded against all odds. Just one more reason for me to be a proud younger sister.

~ **Uchenna Jones Conley, M.D.**
Sister of Jolanda Jones
Los Angeles, California

Jolanda Jones is the perfect person to write this book. If there has been anyone who had to own their S.H.I.T!, it has been my mother. She has had to overcome more things than most people I know or read about. She has had to overcome being raped by her uncle, my grandfather killing himself, poverty, and many other things that would crush anyone else. Many people like using "crutches" in life. Jolanda Jones is NOT one of those people. She raised me to understand my problems and accept them so that I can be the best man possible. Before reading this book, you should decide whether or not you want to take a look in the mirror. This book is not for someone who blames others or is not ready to see that the problem is his or her own self. Owning My S.H.I.T! is exactly what the title states, taking who you are and accepting that person, so you may overcome your "S.H.I.T!". This book is the epitome of how my mother raised me and just as she raised me, she will help you realize your full potential and pull no punches. If you are ready to look at yourself then you are ready for this book. Get ready, set, OWN YOUR S.H.I.T!!

~Jiovanni Jones
Son of Jolanda Jones
Houston, Texas

Jolanda is the strongest willed person I have ever known. I remember a time in high school when Jolanda experienced racism firsthand. The reason this stuck out with me is because I'm a red-headed White male with freckles. We were at a track meet in a small town outside of Houston. Jolanda and some of the girls went to a country store and the owner picked out Jolanda from the group and made a racist comment. Jo was one of the few Black people at Elsik. She came back to the track meet and found me while I was warming up for my race. She was in tears and explained how this had never happened to her before and she was having trouble dealing with it. The experience had a profound impact on both of us. I'd asked Jo to prom because nobody asked her to go and I was shy and too afraid to ask the girl I liked, to go to prom with me. When I went to pick her up for prom, at her friend's house where she was staying, she had just finished winning the state track meet - by herself. I didn't tell my dad I was taking Jo to prom and she didn't tell her mom. We snuck out and went together. We knew our parents wouldn't understand. As I've observed Jolanda grow and mature all these years later, I think she has definitely learned to deal with whatever life may bring and now owns her own S.H.I.T!. I'm looking forward to seeing the other S.H.I.T! Jo has overcome, and I hope you will learn some of what I've known her to be for almost 40 years. Not only is she strong-willed, but she's a strong woman.

~Troy Bearden
High School Prom Date
Teammate and Friend
Beaumont, Texas

Before Jolanda and I began dating, we had been friends for over 20 years. The confident Jo, we see today, is not who she always was. I will never forget, Jolanda had just returned from the US Olympic Trials, in Atlanta, and she learned that the girl she was dating had been driving another girl around town in her car. The next thing I know Jolanda is sitting at my kitchen table crying, and with her nose running, about this girl who had cheated on her and was asking what she should do. I'm thinking, wow this girl is a tough world class athlete and lawyer and here she is having a breakdown over this girl who wasn't worth it in the first place. Definitely not the Jolanda we know now. What's so valuable about this book is Jo is willing to put her S.H.I.T! out there and let you smell it. Which in itself is the way she is owning it. Jo is sharing with you how she contributed to these bone-headed decisions. In life, S.H.I.T! never stops coming but "Owning My S.H.I.T!" will help you navigate your S.H.I.T!ty situations, so you can come out smelling like roses.

~**Cherrise Traylor**
Friend of Jolanda for over 25 years
Houston, Texas

I met Jolanda in 2016 when she was elected to the Houston ISD Board of Education. I work in Board Services. She's one of my bosses. I learned very quickly that Jolanda is a force to be reckoned with and she's fair. I always tell people, "You might get offended by Jolanda's delivery - but one thing she will never do is lie to you." I love the fact that Jolanda always fights for the underdog, the wronged, the less fortunate – indiscriminately, me. I've always heard that Jolanda is a beast in the court room. I'm sure Jolanda is a beast at every aspect in life. I see Jolanda as a mentor, someone I aspire to be like. I've taken little parts of what I've learned and seen from her and incorporated them into my daily life. I'm anxious to read about the life journey of the woman that God has placed along this road of mine. I believe she will help you just like she's helped me, and I've only known her for a short time but hope to be in her life forever. I'm proud of her for courageously putting her life out there so the world can see what I've learned in person from her. I imagine that she's going to be as raw and uncut in Owning My S.H.I.T!! as she is in school board meetings. If my belief holds true, then you'd better hang on to your seats because you're going to be in for the read of your lives, but I promise you'll learn and apply that knowledge to your own lives. Her book will go viral just like her school board videos do. I'd bet money on it.

~Yesenia Wences
HISD Board Services
Houston, Texas

Table of Contents

Foreword by
"Olympian of the Century"
Carl Lewis

Boy, I remember meeting Jolanda when she came to the University of Houston as a student-athlete. It was an interesting time, as she joined a team which had numerous current and future Olympians and world champions. First of all, she wasn't the easiest person to get to know. Looking back now, I can see she had a lot of difficulty in her life but at the time, we were all young and didn't understand those things like I do now. I was also dealing with my own challenges and didn't spend as much time with the young athletes as I would have liked to. But as time went by, it seemed like she had a drive to be successful. I understood where she came from because I used to live right by her high school, in Alief. Actually, I remember when they built it. Being a national class scholar-athlete is very difficult. I saw how hard she had to work, having to go to class, practice, study and travel.

I know from my life and successes that you have to decide how good you want to be. I remember Jolanda talking about wanting to be a lawyer and always talking about her academics more than most athletes. She did talk a lot though... But she was always very inquisitive about everything. Although I was already out of school, at UH, by the time Jolanda arrived on a full-scholarship, I was still training there and competing professionally. So, we saw each other every day at practice. We were also teammates on various USA teams at international competitions. I remember how she liked to talk about the next level and how successful she was going to be. I know some people talked about how she was so aggressive about what she wanted to accomplish, but I understood how you have to speak and work your success into existence.

I feel the most challenging time was cutting her career short. She was a multiple national champion who just walked away and disappeared. She was only 23 years old. Coach Tellez, our coach, always talked about how Jolanda never achieved her full athletic potential. He thought she should have not only made the Olympic Team, but she should have even medaled. She never accomplished either. We never knew why. One thing I always never wanted to do was to have regrets or to ask myself what I could have done differently. I wondered what she was thinking. If she ever had regrets. I thought she was crazy, but we were not aware of the challenges she had to face and conquer. She never shared any of her struggles.

She was distant. In 1999, I moved away to California and New Jersey, my home state, for a number of years. To my surprise, I'm watching TV one day and I see an ad for the reality show Survivor and Jo's on it! When I would visit Houston and attend UH football games, there she was, marching into the Presidential and other VIP suites, invited as a special guest of the university, and go figure, she was a city council member, seriously? Jolanda is one of those people where you know she's going to be somebody but you're just not sure what she's going to be. But what she turned out to be is a very successful person. Jo is a friend who you just don't know where she is going to show up, but wherever it is she's going to be somewhere in charge. Her story is our story, my story. She's had more challenges than most of us could handle but she's managed to figure out a way to overcome despite her hardships. Jo should be angry but instead she's turned her anger into the energy she needs to succeed. When I retired, I used to talk about how I had a great time… and that I'd be pulling knives out of my back for years to come because success brings out haters. I truly admire how Jolanda has found success, love and happiness. She didn't seem that happy when she was younger. It's interesting how our little old lives joined in the hot sun, 34 years ago, on a red track as two young people dreaming. And now she is my lawyer, go figure?

Who would've thought that we would be where we are now, in 2018. But here she is, through it all, still standing and thriving. Her book, this book, Owning My S.H.I.T!, I'm certain will answer a lot of my questions about why she just walked away from an Olympic career that seemed inevitable. I'm hopeful she'll explain why she was so hard to understand and so serious at a time when most young people were relaxing and having fun. I have a feeling that the Jolanda I know will be no nonsense in owning her S.H.I.T!, and I expect nothing less. So here's to the future which is so bright… But first let's look at Jolanda's past so we can learn, love, laugh, cry and be thankful because, after all these years, she's still standing.

Suffering Hardship Internalizing Trauma

Introduction

S.H.I.T!

Suffering Hardship Internalizing Trauma

A hometown hero…
All-American basketball and track athlete…
Four-time national track and field champion…
Member of multiple Halls of Fame for sports and
academics…
Houston City Council member …
Houston School Board member …
Respected criminal defense lawyer …
TV personality, Survivor Palau cast member & star of Sisters
in Law …
Respected legal analyst and author …
Civil rights activist …
Criminal justice activist …
Black power activist …
LGBTQ activist …
Affordable housing activist …
Domestic violence expert and survivor…
Sexual assault survivor …
Record breaker …
Entrepreneur …
Patent owner …
And a recognized public speaker!

As you can see, my resume is impeccable, and I'm no
stranger to the limelight. I'm sure from the looks of my

accomplishments, it would appear that my life has been great. You would think I grew up in the suburbs, with two loving parents, living the American dream. Two parents who were very much invested in my dreams, education, aspirations, inspirations and future goals. To achieve all that I have achieved within the years of my life, it would appear that I have always been blessed to stand on a solid foundation built on love, trust, hard work, and success. I mean how could someone have a S.H.I.T!ty life and manage to become an upstanding woman who defies all odds? Realistically it would seem impossible, but nothing is impossible when you are determined to live your best life despite hardships and trauma.

Unbeknownst to many, I have traveled some very dark and lonely roads. Roads that caused insurmountable S.H.I.T! pile ups throughout my life. During those times, I didn't quite understand what was going on or how to verbalize it, but today I understand that I was **S**uffering **H**ardships while **I**nternalizing **T**rauma. I encountered so much S.H.I.T! that, had I not actually lived through it, I would've never believed that much heartbreak and devastation could befall one person. It didn't make sense and it wasn't fair.

Today, I am prepared to unapologetically expose the demons and secrets that attempted to take my life, thwart my purpose and break my confidence. To encourage those who have experienced or are currently experiencing overwhelming S.H.I.T! that they can't seem to overcome. Let me say, I get it; I've walked in many of your shoes. For those who believe I'm too graphic and should keep my secrets to myself; that it's nobody's business but my own, I will not apologize nor, will I remain silent. This is my truth. Perhaps life hasn't traumatized you as it has me and others, but our struggles are real and the secrecy of them is what keeps us stuck. Our S.H.I.T! must be identified and dealt with honestly.

We've experienced unimaginable horror and trauma and sometimes it's helpful to know that we are not in this alone. That we are not the only people to experience these potentially debilitating and life altering events. I am not and will not act like I'm Miss Manners or Miss Etiquette. The truth matters and it's not my fault or cross to bear if some people can't handle the truth. I am who God created me to be. I choose to believe that He allowed the hardships in my life, so that I could evolve into a beast on the court, on the track, in the courtroom, in public office or wherever else I so choose.

My book, this book, is not intended to make you feel comfortable or to allow you to wallow in self-pity. This book is NOT for that man or that woman who desires to stay stuck. This book is intended to share some of my very painful and personal experiences, that most people would keep secret and feel ashamed of, with the hope that the tools and skill sets I discovered to deal with them might be helpful to you in identifying, accepting and working through your hardships and traumas. Perhaps it could be your road map to work through the extreme discomfort while dealing authentically and honestly with yourself and your S.H.I.T!

The goal is to help you with this process, so that positive change can manifest in your life, as it did in mine. You must be willing to deal with the truth, the whole truth and nothing but the truth, so help you God! If you are willing to TRUTHFULLY deal with your S.H.I.T!, then keep reading. If not, thank you for purchasing your copy and feel free to close it, burn it or put in on the shelf until you are ready, or not.

Let me be brutally honest, my TRUTH is sometimes gut-wrenching, unbelievable, horrifying, devastating, nasty, dirty, stinky and most of all shocking, but it happened and there's no changing these events! That water is under the bridge. Those egg shells have already been broken. That horse has left the barn. Moving forward, however, I decided how to respond to these I-wish-they-never-happened-to-me events. You too have that option. I choose not to be defined by the S.H.I.T! that happened to me. Instead, I choose to be defined by how I respond to my S.H.I.T! What's your response? What is your S.H.I.T!?

I have been told, more times than I can remember, that I shouldn't "harp" on all the negatives of my life; that I should rightfully bury the past and never look back. But oh no, NEVER will I forget my past lest I am doomed to repeat it. I've come to learn that my pain has a positive, powerful purpose! When I share my story across the United States, people are amazed that I'm still alive or better yet, in my right mind. They have told me for decades that I need to write a book; that my story is inspiring; that I can help people. This book is my response to their requests.

Statistically, I shouldn't be where I am. I could be totally messed up, right here, right now! I could have been that person who did drugs to drown out my life, my memories and my pain like some of my family members. Rather than using drugs to distract me from my purpose, success was and still is, my drug of choice, to help me live a happy, productive, purpose-filled life. Prison could have been a part of my story too, like various family members. I could have been that homeless person, you pass by every day and refuse to look at, simply because life beat me down and I could not find my way back up, like other people I know. Better yet, I could be six feet under and only a memory, like my dad and two uncles, who took their own lives; or like my brother, aunt, and numerous cousins, who were murdered. They were victims of the street. I could have been a single welfare mom, depending on the system, like other family members.

By no means do I intend to demean anyone who could have or should have or would have been something other than they are today due to their S.H.I.T! I have come to realize that

I was called to be an advocate for these very same people. I have been consistently told by others that I was chosen to be a beacon of light and ray of hope for those who think they cannot succeed due to lack of parental involvement, lack of resources, lack of support, or a lack of whatever, you fill in the blank. I rejected that calling initially but have now accepted that there may be some truth to it. These people, we people, have a voice and our voices matter, but our voices and our choices have been drowned out and buried deep below our piles of S.H.I.T!

It is my sincere belief that God created me to endure unbelievable and seemingly insurmountable hardships, so that I could understand and empathize with the hearts, minds and circumstances of those who repeatedly internalize their trauma. I believe that God allowed me to internalize my own trauma, to teach me, albeit very painful learning lessons, for the express purpose of understanding how damaging internalizing trauma is. It also allowed me to figure out how not to internalize and how to face the trauma and hardships head on, either alone or with the help of others who love and support me. From the depths of my soul, I believe that we, as individuals, desire to do right and to be right, but the S.H.I.T! that takes place during our journey of life, often causes us to hold or fold. There is another option and that is what this book is about.

When I honestly look back over my life, there was one thing that caused everything to be chaotic ... LOVE or the lack thereof! Love is a powerful force to be reckoned with because it will either make you or break you. In my case it broke me, and I mean into a bunch of pieces. But I thank God that He is the potter and I am the clay and He knew how and when to put my pieces back together.

You see, when we fail to receive love, especially as children, during those crucial times of development, it shifts our world into a cycle of dysfunction that is hard to deviate from. Notice, I said "hard" not "impossible". Let's be real, how many people, places and things have you blamed for the S.H.I.T! in your life? When, if you truly step back, sit down, actively listen and be quiet… you will find that **love or the lack thereof** has been the culprit every time.

When I realized what the missing element was for me, then and only then, was I able to stand in my authentic truth and nakedness and take ownership of my S.H.I.T! Not my mother's S.H.I.T!, not my father's S.H.I.T!, not my ex-husband's S.H.I.T!, but Jolanda's S.H.I.T! Now, don't get me wrong, they contributed to my S.H.I.T!, but I had to choose to no longer give them power over my life nor my love for myself… a powerful revelation taught to me by my Grand Mommy, Claudina Jones, known lovingly as "Dear".

Let's be clear…I got through my S.H.I.T! by owning my S.H.I.T! but it was a process. I had to first learn to identify my S.H.I.T! before I could figure out how to deal and work through my S.H.I.T! which would then allow me to own my S.H.I.T!! Once I owned my S.H.I.T! nobody could out my S.H.I.T!! Now, I wish somebody would! They will find out quickly, and probably uncomfortably, how I deal with people who try to get into my S.H.I.T!! Owning my S.H.I.T! is and has been my most empowering decision.

I took ownership of the parts I played in the chapters of my life, whether good or bad. Yes, I am very successful today, but it required me to do some very difficult work. Self-analysis! I had to come face to face with my S.H.I.T!ty situations, circumstances, lies, deceptions, self-rejection, self-denial, parental abandonment, abuse and so much more. But ultimately, I had to choose me, and though not easy, I made it through those very deep dark trenches. I came out on the other side. I am hopeful that *"Owning My S.H.I.T!"* will help you step out of the dark pits of life and into your own shining light.

Many have seen me on the news, speaking on different platforms, on "Sisters in Law" and "Survivor", but this book is me naked and unashamed. It is me, Jolanda Jones, being unapologetic, uncut and unafraid!

I am unapologetically free to be me today and I love it! It wasn't always this way. I used to live in fear that someone would out my S.H.I.T! and it would all be revealed. Well, once you learn to own your S.H.I.T!, no one can use your S.H.I.T! as a weapon against you. My prayer is that you will not only focus on my S.H.I.T!, but that you will be encouraged to and actually face your own S.H.I.T!, with the hopes of being set FREE and being the best purpose-filled person that you can be!

I am convinced that you are going to love your new-found freedom and unapologetic-self! So, if you are ready to *Own Your S.H.I.T!*, like I have learned to own mine, then please continue this journey with me. Travel with me on the road to becoming your best self, by using your S.H.I.T!, like cow manure is used to fertilize plants, to necessarily fertilize your positive growth into the best and most productive person you can be. And by living the best and most fulfilled life you can live!

Respectfully,
Jolanda

Chapter One
Daddy Go Bang!

After my dad killed himself with me in the room with him, I used to run around saying "Daddy go bang!"

Let me go back. I was born to John and Gwendolyn Jones in 1965. Two young love-birds who married in their teens and chose to start a life together in Third Ward, Houston, Texas. We lived on my grandparents' property, in an upstairs unit of a four-plex, located in the middle portion of the family lot. My father was a very strong, kind and intellectual man. He was a United States Marine during the Vietnam era. According to my mother and those who knew him, he did not return as the same man, who left. I can't imagine the things that he witnessed and the mental and emotional toll it took on him as a teenager in a war, but whatever he witnessed primed him to take his life less than five years after he discharged from the military. Upon his return, he was very distant, isolated and cried all the time.

Prior to enlisting he was not the type of man that would randomly cry. He was the definition of cool, calm and collected. He was a six foot four inches tall and muscular. He was incredibly handsome and wickedly smart, so much so, that he graduated from high school at 16. He was an artist and attended Texas Southern University. He studied under the renowned artist Dr. John Biggers. His canvasses were his heaven, yet his heaven didn't pay his bills. He had a wife and child to support.

He struggled with living up to his father's expectations. He wanted nothing more than to make his dad proud but it would never be. My grandfather was an impossible man to please. I haven't found one person who told me my grandfather was proud of him. Curiously, one of the few people my grandfather was ever nice to was me. I firmly believe it was because he felt guilty about my dad's death, being that he was partly responsible for it. My father was admired by many, especially by his younger brothers, who wanted nothing more than to be like him. From the looks of it all, one would think that the sky was the limit for my dad, but his actions would soon make it plain that he was battling undiagnosed mental illness, that was deeply rooted in pain; the depths of which were obviously hidden beyond the comprehension of those who loved him. He was drowning and no one either recognized it or knew how to throw him the life jacket he needed.

To earn a living, my dad worked at Big J's Lounge, the café that his parents owned, where people gathered, ate, drank, danced and played pool. He was the keeper-of-the-peace, what we now call a bouncer. The café was located on the very back of the family lot. He wanted to work for his dad's side business, a cab company but wasn't allowed to. My grandfather also owned Square Deal Paint and Body Shop, which is one way my granddad acquired his own cars. When customers didn't pay, he kept their cars. My dad didn't work for his dad because he was never paid his worth.

My dad also wanted to stay in school at TSU but he couldn't afford tuition. The GI Bill didn't cover it. My dad reached an agreement with his dad, to purchase one of his cars, so that he could own his own cab and be his own boss. When my dad paid the agreed upon purchase price, my grandfather refused to honor the agreement. My dad was devastated.

Thanksgiving had just passed and Christmas was on its way. They, he and my mom, didn't have enough money to buy food for Thanksgiving. My mom's parents had bought the groceries for my mom to prepare Thanksgiving dinner. My dad was frustrated and embarrassed. Right after this, is when my dad killed himself. On that night, in early December 1966, he was very upset and wanted to speak with his sister Bridget, who was living with their parents. He walked past our apartment to get to my grandparents' house to reach Aunt Bridget, but she was asleep. For whatever reason, no one woke her up so he left, and walked back to our apartment.

When he walked into the apartment, he was crying and talking to himself. My mother had just finished cooking dinner. I was in the baby bed sound asleep. My mom tried to console him; to calm him down but he wasn't having any of that. He just wanted to be able to work and earn enough money to take care of his family. He was 21 years old and had a lot of responsibilities.

He was complaining about his dad not allowing him to drive a cab for him, so he could earn money to take care of us. He walked into the bedroom where my mom and I were. After he explained to my mom why he was upset, she remembered that he had not eaten so she went to fix his plate. She had prepared stew that night. As she left the bedroom to go fix his plate, he said something about "doing something for us to help us". As she prepared his plate, she saw him sitting on the bed, still crying, and surprisingly he had "that gun" in his hand. She hadn't seen him come into the apartment with that gun, so she couldn't figure out where he'd gotten it from. The next thing she heard was a loud "thud". She distinctly didn't hear a gunshot like the one she heard when he'd accidently discharged that gun before. She hurried into the room and found my dad slumped over. He'd shot himself with "that gun". How did he shoot himself with "that gun? "That gun" was supposed to be at "Mr. Willie Jones' house". My mom always called her father-in-law, "Mr. Willie Jones."

The story behind "that gun" was an incident that scared my mom to death. About a week prior, my dad had come home, one night after working at the café. He was angry because there had been a fight and to break the fight up, he tried to shoot "that gun" into the air. "That gun" jammed and didn't shoot. The fight got out of hand. When he came home that night, he'd brought "that gun" into the bedroom and was complaining, to my mom, about how it wouldn't fire. I was in my baby bed. He was demonstrating as he spoke. It was then that that gun went off accidently between their bed and my baby bed, which was a very small distance. That terrified my mom. I could've been shot. She could've been shot. My dad could've been shot. My mom begged my dad to get "that gun" out of the house. That gun didn't belong to him and should never have been in the apartment anyway. It was my grandfather's and was normally kept in the café. She told him "take it to Mr. Willie Jones' house". He complied, or so she thought.

My dad had fallen off the bed onto the floor. He was in his underwear, with his clothes folded neatly. His eyes rolled back into his head. There was blood, and what she thinks was brain matter, on the white sheets. Before the night ended, his blood and brain matter were on the duster she was wearing too. It was also on my grandmother's blouse, which interestingly, my grandmother eventually gave me as a family heirloom.

In shock and total panic, my mom rushed out of the apartment, forgetting to take me with her, to get my grandmother, who was a licensed vocational nurse. My mom was 20 years old. My heart hurts, right now just thinking of the pain and devastation she felt, finding her husband, the man she loved, her child's father, shot in the head, either unconscious or dead, by his own hand, with "that gun" that wasn't supposed to be in our apartment.

My grandmother, my Uncle Rodney, and Aunt Bridget ran to our apartment. Unfortunately, there was nothing anybody could do. My grandmother tried to make my dad as comfortable as possible until the ambulance got there. Dear screamed at my Uncle Roscoe, to hurry up and call the paramedics. Uncle Roscoe called and came back and told Dear that the paramedics were not coming. He said they told him why did they need to come since my dad shot himself in the head. That's when my grandmother jumped into action and told my mom, aunt and uncle that they'd have to take my dad to the hospital themselves.

The shock in the room was at an all-time high. Everyone was crying, screaming, and praying, while trying to figure out how to get him down the stairs, into the car and to Ben Taub Hospital. Can you imagine the pressure and desperation of trying to save my dad? He was unresponsive, blood gushing from his head wound, gasping for breaths that grew shorter and shorter with each passing moment.

My father's big stature made the task of carrying him down the stairs extremely difficult. During the move from the bedroom, down the stairs and into the car, blood was everywhere. Aunt Bridget carried his shoulders and head. Uncle Rodney carried his lower body. Uncle Rodney told me my dad was hard to carry because he was slippery from the blood being everywhere.

Consequently, Aunt Bridget my dad's head slipped out of her arms and hit the window seal. She was upset about dropping his head and was extremely careful not to do it again as they descended the stairs. The blood on the window seal stayed there for years. It was a constant reminder of what happened to my dad and a constant tool used to torment be by bullies during my childhood, until the four-plex was eventually torn down.

They finally got my dad into the car, left me with Uncle Roscoe, and took off, like a bat out of hell, trying to get him to Ben Taub. My grandmother prayed the rosary the whole ride.

We were devout Catholics. The rosary was supposed to protect us from evil. My mom frantically yelled for my dad to just hold on and prayed the entire way there. They drove from McGowan, to Scott, to North MacGregor, to Ben Taub Hospital. My grandmother believes my dad took his last breath on North MacGregor, not ten minutes from Ben Taub Hospital, and two minutes from where I live today. My dad took his last breath with his head in my mom's arms. As they continued to drive, from the moment of his last breath, they suspected he was dead. That last portion of the drive, when they knew in their gut that he was dead, was such a feeling of helplessness and desperation. Prior to that, there was hope that the doctors could save him.

To this day, I am angry about my family having to rush my dad to the hospital by themselves. They shouldn't have had to endure the grueling task of watching him die right before their eyes. As my dad's daughter, I am angry that people who were experts in saving lives refused to come and try and save him. For the longest time, I wondered "what if" they had just come, would they have saved his life? Would my life be different? Would I have a dad?

My dad died that night, never knowing that a piece of my mom died with him. He will never know that the hole in his head, that took his life, left a bleeding hole in my heart, that would attempt to take my life as well.

My dad didn't leave a note. My mom, and others, believe that my dad thought by killing himself that he was worth more to our family dead than alive. In addition to him making the statement about doing something good for our family the night he killed himself, he had had previous conversations with others talking about the benefits my mom and I would get, from the Veterans Administration, if he were dead. No one suspected that he was actually considering suicide. Sadly, my mom received a whopping approximately

$36 per month in VA benefits for me until I was 18. I got a raise at 18 and received approximately $61 per month until I turned 21. That was what my dad's death actually translated into for my mother and me. Pathetic.

My normal was always knowing my dad killed himself. I got teased a lot, about it, by friends. I was told constantly that "you crazy just like yo daddy." Some kids would gang up and chant it. It made me sad. Or they would say, "go die like yo daddy," when they wanted to make fun of me. I didn't know anyone else whose dad had killed himself. I was the only one. Or they would taunt me, often pointing to the blood spot on the window seal. Sometimes when we played outside and I might have to walk by the four-plex, it was not uncommon to hear, "ah, ha, yo daddy's head is under the bed!" That always scared me, and I would stand frozen, afraid to pass the four-plex for fear my dad's head would come out and kill me or give me a heart attack. "You ain't got no daddy!" was also a common taunt. I was the butt of jokes about my dad whenever anybody wanted to hurt my feelings. It was a miserable and hopeless existence that no child should have to go through.

When I was old enough to understand suicide, I had nightmares about my dad's suicide constantly. The recurring dream went something like this: He and I were always being chased by people or monsters who wanted to harm us. We ran frantically and desperately together trying to get away. They would always eventually catch and kill my dad and eventually they would always either catch me or be about to catch or kill me and I would always wake up gasping for air right before I died or got caught. I was always sleep deprived. To this day, I don't sleep well. I try not to sleep so deeply because I don't want to dream.

As an adult, I struggled with deciding whether to undergo hypnosis, to try and have my own personal memories of my dad. People who knew my dad, always told me that he loved me and took me everywhere with him. Although that sounded nice, I struggled with believing that he loved me as much as they said he did because "if he loved me so much then why did he leave me?" Dear always said, until the day she died, that the two people he loved more than life itself were her and me. And the only explanation that made sense, to her, was that whatever pain he felt, the night he committed suicide, must've been so great that it blocked his ability to think about his love for her or me; that, had he thought of either of us, he would've never pulled the trigger.

I was so desperate for my own personal memories of my dad, that if I learned that someone knew my dad, I would immediately try to locate them and ask them about him. I learned my current across-the-street-neighbor, Maryann Young, was an art student with my dad at TSU. Before I knew it, I had cornered her in her front yard and interrogated her about my dad. Thankfully, she was nice enough to share everything she remembered about him and was tickled pink that I was his daughter, because she never knew that fact. She said that all the TSU art students looked up to him because he was such a talented artist, super nice, and on a personal note, that he was very handsome. When I learned, within the last year, that my dad enlisted in the military, with a group of six neighborhood friends and only two got in, my dad and his best friend, Darrin Voshay. I friended Mr. Voshay on Facebook, asked him questions via Facebook. At some point he trusted me enough to give me his phone number and I was actually able to speak with him about my dad. I am thankful. He shared that he'd always wondered about me and kept up with me through the media. There are other examples of my unquenchable hunger to learn more about my dad through people I learn knew him, but regardless of the details of his life that I learn, there lives in me, an endless void.

So, the question for me was: how to deal with my constant need to have my dad's love and validation when it is physically and emotionally impossible? I had to seek, and ultimately ask for, professional mental health help to figure out how to fill the void.

I found the courage to contact a mental health provider and ask for help. I was sick and tired of feeling sorry for myself and making unhealthy decisions because I didn't have a daddy. I'm no longer ashamed that my dad killed himself. With the help of a mental health professional, I learned and accepted that I had nothing to do with his suicide. My dad alone made that very bad and short-sighted decision. While I wish he hadn't killed himself, no amount of wishing will bring him back so I can either feel sorry for myself for as long as this situation persists, which is forever, or I can choose to move forward and figure out how to love myself, regardless of me not having a dad. I own that he'll never be around to give me whatever I believed he should've given or taught me. I own that him committing suicide doesn't determine my innate value, one way or the other. I own that his decision to kill himself was his decision to make. I own that if someone is ignorant or stupid enough to blame me for my father's fateful decision then they shouldn't be permitted, by me, to be in my world.

Suffering Hardship Internalizing Trauma

Chapter Two

That Bastard!
I Never Liked Him Anyway

When it was just my mom and me, and she was trying to juggle being a single-mom, while attending and ultimately graduating from TSU, she needed the support of her network of friends and family to help babysit me. She only left me with people she trusted. The family could be trusted, or so she thought. My mom was the oldest of four girls. My mom was the first, of the West girls to move out and get married. One of my mother's sisters had my cousin next to me with a married man. So, she ended up being a single parent. Eventually that aunt met and married a man from out of town. For the purposes of this book, let's just call that man Shawn. He was approximately six foot, seven inches tall. He came from a family of extremely tall brothers. Shawn ended up being my uncle through marriage.

At the time, my cousin and I were the only two grandchildren. I was the oldest. For the longest time, it was just the two of us. Our moms let us play together and bathe together. It was no big deal. At the time my aunt, husband and cousin lived in some apartments in Third Ward. It was there that I first remember Shawn trying to separate my cousin and me. One time my cousin and I were in the tub together getting bathed and playing with bubbles. Shawn yelled that boys and girls weren't supposed to bathe together and took me out of the tub. I didn't understand what all the commotion was about, but my cousin and I never bathed together again.

I don't know how it came about but somehow Shawn sometimes babysat me. I remember the layout of the room where he abused me like it was yesterday. I always knew that I was abused in the Married Dorms at TSU, which used to sit where the Barbara Jordan Mickey Leland School of Public Affairs, currently sits. After talking with my mom and a family friend recently, we were able to figure out whose dorm room it was and that I was between three and four years old when it started, and that it ended when I was five or six. Uncle Shawn was a giant. He was the biggest of all of the grown-ups and I was a little girl. He forced himself on me. He tried to put his big penis into my little vagina. It hurt so bad. It used to burn when I used the restroom afterwards. He also forced his penis into my mouth and squirted this white stuff down my throat. It had a stinky smell and nasty taste. It made me gag and throw up. He threatened me not to tell anyone or else he would kill me and my mom. I was terrified and afraid. So, I didn't tell anyone. I didn't want him to kill me. I didn't want him to kill my mom either. I kept the secret. I hated when I had to go with him. At some point Uncle Shawn moved back to his home town and I never had to see him again. My memories of him faded away over time.

In my late teens, I started dating and was pressured to have sex with my boyfriend. Before I actually had sex, my boyfriend would foreplay and whenever I saw or smelled pre-ejaculate or semen, I got physically nauseous, but I couldn't figure out why. Sex with my boyfriend was never enjoyable. It always hurt. I didn't lubricate like I was told I was supposed to. A sick feeling always came over me. Everything in my body clammed up. I was sick and had problems keeping my stomach settled and food down. It was like my body was trying to protect itself from harm. It was weird. I'd heard sex was supposed to be enjoyable and fulfilling, but all I ever felt was discomfort, pain and trepidation.

At 21 years old, while in college, the memories of Uncle Shawn's sexual abuse of me flooded back. All of a sudden, the pieces of my memories came together, and everything made sense. It was my dirty little secret. I was ashamed. It was his fault that I had problems with sex; that I never had orgasms; that it was always painful. Interestingly, prior to my painful memories returning, I'd taken a Human Sexuality class at UH and had self-diagnosed that I was anorgasmic. In my mind, I was just one of those people who couldn't have a sexual orgasm like I read about in books. Years later, I would learn that I misdiagnosed myself.

Once the memories of my uncle's molestation of me came back, I needed someone to talk to. My first thought was my mom but we never really had a close relationship. Besides that, she wasn't someone I felt would have my back no matter what, especially for something so intimate and personal. For some inexplicable reason, the first person I told was Mama Harriet. She believed me. I was relieved. The first words she spoke in response to my reveal, still sticks with me today, she growled matter of factly, "That bastard! I never liked him anyway." She said everything made sense now. That's why Uncle Shawn always complained about how close my cousin and I were. We weren't allowed to be inseparable anymore. Mama Harriet also said that must've been why I always stayed close to Uchenna when Uncle Shawn was around her. I was protecting my baby sister from that "bastard"; that "pervert, raping her granddaughter". I remember that conversation vividly. Now that I'm a criminal defense lawyer, I recognize that his behavior towards me is defined as grooming. He definitely groomed me.

After speaking with Mama Harriet, I realized it wasn't my fault. Although I was a child at the time, that hadn't stopped me from believing that his abuse of me was somehow my fault. We, victims, often times blame ourselves for things that we have no control over. Mama Harriet helped me understand that it was Uncle Shawn's fault and his fault alone and I was only a child. He was a predator of the worst kind. I did well surviving and finding success notwithstanding his brutality.

From Mama Harriet, I got the courage to tell my mom, although I didn't know if she'd believe me, but I felt that, as my mom, she should know. When I told her, she believed me. I was pleasantly surprised. She apologized to me for not protecting me from Uncle Shawn. She wished I'd told her, but she understood that I was only a kid. I explained that I was terrified of him killing both of us. It was my mom who suggested that I tell my aunt. I felt uncomfortable telling her too. She'd had two children with Uncle Shawn. They were my cousins and I loved them. More importantly, he was their dad and they loved him. Even though he'd moved back to his home town long before I told anyone, I was still afraid, I didn't want to cause family drama. I didn't want my cousins to be mad at me. I didn't want my cousins to think I was lying on their dad. I also believe that since it took me so long to say anything, people wouldn't believe me.

I got up the courage to tell my aunt. She listened. She, too, apologized to me for what Uncle Shawn did to me and for not protecting me. She said she didn't know. If only she'd known. My secret was out, albeit to only Mama Harriet, my mom and aunt. I thought that demon was exorcized. I was wrong.

I continued to have problems sexually and with intimacy. I continued to fake enjoying sex. There was so much pressure associated with sex. Whoever your partner was always asked if it was good. What was I supposed to say? No, I feel nauseated and want to throw up. You're hurting me. Can we please stop? I was raped by my uncle and I don't enjoy sex. Nope, I didn't say any of that. I just made whatever noises I'd seen on television about what good sex was supposed to sound like and kept it moving. I felt destined to never enjoy sex in my life. Damnit Uncle Shawn, how did you take something that was supposed to so be beautiful away from me and doom me to a life with no authentic intimacy or enjoyment?!

An either painful sex life or non-existent sex life was the norm. I thought I was fine. I continued to be successful and no longer really thought about Uncle Shawn, at all. I didn't tell my cousins because I thought everything was fine. Then Uncle Shawn's brother died. I was in my forties. I literally hadn't seen or been afraid of Uncle Shawn in decades. Quite frankly, I never even thought of him. To my knowledge, he still lived in his home town. When it came time for his brother's funeral, I felt like I owed it to his brother to pay my respects. Besides that, everybody liked Uncle Shawn's brother. Our family knew his wife and their children. He was nice and didn't do anything to anyone. So I went.

While at his wake, one of his brothers walked up to me to speak and I freaked out. I started sweating and my heart felt like it was pounding outside of my chest. I felt like I was having a heart attack. I could hardly breath. I yelled for him to get away from me; to not touch me. I thought he was Uncle Shawn. I wasn't going to let him hurt me anymore. Despite my age and success, I still felt like a child fighting for my life. He kept trying to calm me down; imploring me that he wasn't Uncle Shawn. In fact, he promised me that he wasn't Uncle Shawn. I didn't believe him. I pushed him away. Finally, someone came back to where we were and verified to me that he actually wasn't Uncle Shawn; that he was one of Uncle Shawn's brothers. I was shaken and confused. I was convinced that I would know him if I ever saw him again. I mean he abused me for years. I didn't understand what had just happened. I had no idea that Uncle Shawn, or someone I thought was Uncle Shawn, would still have such a profound effect on me. Hell, I was a successful and accomplished woman. I hadn't thought about Uncle Shawn in decades. At some point I got tired of trying to figure out what happened, and I just left the wake.

My response to Uncle Shawn forced me to accept that notwithstanding the nearly forty-year separation of his abuse of me that I still hadn't dealt with it; that it still affects me. I had to own that not thinking about S.H.I.T!; that pushing S.H.I.T! to the back of your mind, doesn't fix the problem. I had to own that success doesn't make problems disappear. Respect by your community does not make the pain and fear go away. I had to own that I never wanted to have a melt down in public again over my uncle sexually assaulting me. I also had to own the fact that sharing was therapeutic. It empowered me because it helped me to place the blame and shame where it belongs, on the perpetrator. Interestingly, it literally allowed me to wash the stench off of me and throw it onto him. I freed myself of the "victim" label and claimed the "victor" label.

I absolutely believe that me sharing the details of my uncle's molestation of me is helpful. It warns parents that relatives aren't always trustworthy. If me sharing my story makes one parent pay closer attention to their children's responses to people around them then it's worth it. Me sharing what he did to me with my grandmother allowed her to connect dots. She now knew that I was trying to protect my sister from Uncle Shawn. So hopefully, some parent reading this, when they observe certain behavior with their kids, may ask their children a question and be able to stop abuse and prevent further abuse in the future.

Chapter Three

Lingering Chasm of Dysfunction

It is a proven fact that death and life work hand in hand. When my father died, that was the end of his life, but those connected to him, had to learn to live on. We had to learn a new way of living life without him and how to rebound from the impact he made during his time on the earth as a son, brother, husband, friend and most of all, as my father. My mom, only twenty years old at the time, had to live with the mind-blowing reality that she was a single mother through no fault of her own.

My mom never intended on being a single mom, working or going to college. Her dream was to be my dad's wife, make babies with him and live happily ever after. Yet, before their dream got going well, their dreams were gone, and she was now in a single motherhood nightmare.

My parents started dating when my mom was a student at Fidelity Manor High School. She was 15 years old, in the 10th grade and my dad was 16 years old, and in college. He studied art and was super smart. I was told that he had Mensa-level intelligence. My mom's grades were important to her only because of my father. He was so determined to have a smart wife that when he was in the Marines, believe this or not, he actually required my mom to send him her report cards, with the expectation of seeing A's and B's, because "C's" were unacceptable. He dreamed of having a smart wife. Since my mom dreamed of being his wife, A's and B's it was.

My dad's educational expectations for my mom conflicted, at least initially, with hers. She had major reservations about going to college, in fact she was deadset against it. In her opinion, college women and sorority women were snobbish. An opinion my mom arrived at because of her mom, Mama Harriet.

Per my mom, Mama Harriet majored in English, pledged a sorority Zeta Phi Beta, and graduated from Wiley College. She quit teaching English, one to be a housewife and two because she had severe arthritis. Since she didn't have to work, she socialized a lot with her friends. When they got together for their Bid Whisk games, or for the Fat Stock Show and Rodeo, they drank beer, with salt on the can, much like they put on margarita glasses today, and talked about people, especially non-college educated, non-business owning, blue collar people. My mom didn't hold the same opinion and especially didn't like that they looked down on people and talked about them. She attributed my grandmother's snobbery to being a sorority girl. Consequently, my mom had no intention of going to college or being in a sorority. This sentiment didn't sit well with my dad. He expected his wife to go to college and make good grades. No wife of his was going to be uneducated so if she expected to marry him, she had better change her plans and go to college. My mom's dreams changed into his dreams. College was her revised destination.

After my dad's suicide, my mom's world as she knew it and the dreams she and my dad had made were gone. Now what? She immediately had to figure out a new normal as a single mom. She also was faced with figuring out how to earn a living and take care of me, all the while grieving my dad's death.

The pain was unbearable, but she had to soldier on. She started looking for jobs and enrolled in college at TSU. She took jobs caring for children at Bunny Land, a private preschool, and at Wheeler Nursery, a daycare. I got to attend both schools because my mom worked there. So, she had no babysitting problems at work. At TSU, it was different. Often times I could attend class with her but during the times I couldn't, her coworkers and various family and friends would watch me while she was in class. Life was tough, but she managed. I never saw my mom cry. I don't believe my mom grieved, nor do I believe she had the time to.

I don't have a lot of happy memories of when I was a little girl. With the exception of my mom loving to dance and using me as her swing out partner, she was the lead (the man) and I followed. There was a stereo with a record player. My mom would put the record on the disc player, lay the needle on either the record or the album, and the music would play. We mostly listened and danced to Stevie Wonder, Maze & Frankie Beverly, Otis Redding; basically, Rhythm and Blues. Us dancing together were my happy memories. To this day, I love to dance and swing out.

While my mom attended TSU, it was always a chore getting to and from school when my mom didn't have a car. First, we lived off of Ardmore, in some red brick apartments with a pool, a frog statute and a whole lot of real frogs. Then we lived off of MacGregor Bayou, in Field Town Apartments, where I remember it snowed in 1972, the year Uchenna was born. I built a snowman. Come to think of it that was a happy memory as well. Before Uchenna, it was just my mom and me. I remember one day she had a Volkswagen and then she didn't. We walked everywhere. Us walking was mostly me hating to have to walk everywhere while being dragged by mom to keep up. Every time I think of that period of my life, I feel like Fred Flintstone moving his feet super-fast to keep up with my mom.

My mom's stride covered much more ground than my toddling footsteps. I have a specific memory of me being no more than three or four years old, tired as hell, wondering when we were going to get there, being dragged by mom to keep up and me wanting to stop but I didn't have a choice. I just had to keep it moving. Someone saw my mom, a barely twenty-something, briskly walking, with me, on the grass along South MacGregor. No bike trails existed then. The person stopped the car and asked my mom if she wanted a ride. Without missing a step or taking her eyes off of our path, my mom answered politely and matter-of-factly, "No, thank you"; and we kept walking! I remember whispering to myself, "take the ride, please mom, take the ride". I knew better than to say a word.

I don't recall my mom dating much. I remember a German she dated. I remember two civil rights icons she dated. For the most part, it was just she and I. I have no memories of her telling me she loved me. She complained a lot about us being in the situation we were in because of my dad. I think she directed her anger at my dad towards me, the only living remnant of him. She was always angry at life and always angry at me.

Considering the circumstances, I thought my mother should've embraced and held on to me for dear life, but she didn't. My father's death and how it occurred caused my mother to enter a dark place. A place where there was little to no room for anyone or anything to pry its way in, especially me. For the longest time, I believed from the depths of my soul, that when my mom looked at me, she saw my father. Her anger and disappointment at his destruction of our family and his betrayal of her, created a lingering chasm of dysfunction. My dad hurt her, so she hurt me.

I don't think my mom ever considered that I was traumatized by my dad's suicide although she clearly knew that she was his victim. I think she believed that I was too young to have been devastated. She thought wrong. I understand her life changed considerably but, she was incapable of appreciating that, I too, was a victim of my dad's S.H.I.T!

In my mind, as a child, I was the most affected, because I was forced to grow up without the love, guidance, direction or protection of my father. I was at the mercy of a mother who loathed me. I believe since she couldn't take her anger out on my dad; she took it out on me. My mom never told me she loved me until I was in my 30's. She told me often that she wished I was never born; that her life would be so much better without me; that I was worthless; and that she wished that she would've aborted me, and that I was just like my dad. What I knew about my dad, from my mom, was that he was a disappointment, changed her life for the worst and her life would've been better had she never met him or had me.

My mom's anger didn't dissipate as time went on. Life kept hitting her hard, she ended up having four more kids after me. For the most part all the baby-daddies of my siblings didn't stick around, nor did they help her financially.

One of my sister's dad was an international Ph.D. student at Rice University. After my mom got pregnant with her, he went back to Nigeria. To this day, neither my mom nor my sister has contact with him. My other sister's dad was and is a lawyer in Houston. Unfortunately for my mom, he chose to marry someone else and had other children after my sister. He gave my mom $100 hundred dollars per year, for my sister, which consisted of $50 dollars for Christmas and $50 dollars for her birthday but NO child support. Just trifling. The only two of my siblings who have the same dad are my brothers.

Their dad was Greg. Greg cheated on my mom and committed acts of domestic abuse and violence against her, in my presence. I remember one time when my mom, who was eight and one half months pregnant with my brother Chuck, drove to where Greg was staying with one of his side-pieces. He'd left my mom pregnant and alone. He wasn't helping financially. My mom was on the porch of the house he was living at. She knocked on the door and begged Greg to please come home with her. His side-piece came outside yelling and called my mom, Uchenna and me, nasty names. She yelled at my mom to take herself and her "ugly ass kids with her". I was ten. Uchenna was three.

Rather than treat my mom respectfully, Greg came onto the porch, yelled at my mom - totally siding with his side-piece - and I shockingly saw him try to kick my mom, in her pregnant stomach. In an effort to dodge his kick, my mom leaned away from the kick and ended up falling down the stairs. She struggled to get up with her huge belly, to get away from Greg's violence and ran back to the car, where Uchenna and I were waiting. My mom sped away crying. I was crying too. I was scared. I didn't like seeing my mom get hurt. No child wants to see her mom get treated like that.

Some of Greg's side-pieces verbally abused my mom and me, sometimes in person, and sometimes by calling our apartment. I remember one of his side-pieces, in particular, calling our apartment, I answered the phone, and she told me to tell my mom that Greg belonged to her and he was staying with her. She called my mom "desperate." She called me "ugly just like my momma" and "little black African with nappy hair". My feelings were so hurt. I was a child and she was an adult. At that time, Greg didn't leave that woman.

Greg and my mom started dating again after the lawyer left. That is how my baby brother came along. The second time around Greg's behavior still didn't change. He was still a whore and continued to abuse my mom and still didn't pay child support. Here we go again, now my mom was a single parent of five kids with no child support from the fathers of my sisters and brothers.

For the most part, the men in my mom's life treated her and us, my siblings and me, disrespectfully. There was only one that half way treated us nice. His name was Basil and he was younger than my mom. He was from Trinidad and Tobago. Other than Basil, my mom's boyfriends didn't support us. All they did was lie to my mom, tell her they loved her and used her. Again, hindsight is 20/20, all they used my mom for, was money and a place to stay. Greg used her for a place to stay, when he didn't have a side-piece taking care of him, and money from her paycheck. No one treated us as if we were their children. Every now and then my baby sister's dad would come and get her.

At the time my mother worked at the post office, which she hated with a passion. She started working there right before Uchenna was born. She always came home tense, angry, exhausted and full of anxiety. Basically, just always in a bad mood. I never looked forward to her coming home from work, because I knew it was going to be some S.H.I.T!! Her mood was so bad that I decided, at an early age, that I wasn't going to work at a job that I hated because miserable moms make miserable kids. I knew I would never work at the post office. Supervisors always harassed the letter carriers. My mom was a carrier.

As the oldest, I was required to cook, clean and care for my siblings when I was the tender age of six years and ten months old. I was responsible for keeping the house or apartment (based on where we lived at the time) in good working order. I was responsible for combing my sibling's hair, getting them dressed and ready for school, and helping them with their homework. I was their constant babysitter. No kid should have to be the primary caregiver of their siblings but, alas, I was. I learned how to take up for and defend others by being the oldest sibling. I didn't want my siblings to get beat by my mother, like I did, so I would offer to take their whippings for them. No matter what, I was always subjected to my mom's lingering internal anger, bitterness, resentment and regrets.

When my mom decided that I was in trouble, which was all of the time, she would always say, "that's what's wrong with you, you're just like your daddy". In my mom's eyes, to be just like my dad was a curse. And her tone necessarily implied that I couldn't help but be a bad person because my dad was bad. Can you imagine having to hear that from your mother your entire childhood? My mind was constantly racing to try and figure out how to please my mom. What did I need to do to make her love me? The emotional torment was endless. The need to please her and try to get her approval was the constant theme in my life, well into my 20's.

I tried to be perfect. I did everything, within my power, to make my mother proud. I tried not to be the constant mistake she'd made with my dad or his tremendous burden on her. I was alive but I often wished I'd died with him. For God's sake, she would tell me she wished "I was never born" because her "life would be so much better without me."

I was a constant reminder of what she lost and of the person who inflicted the cruelest fate of all on her: my dad. Her life and the difficulties of her life were my fault. As my mom's first born, the one who took care of her kids and kept the house running, why couldn't I just have a chance at life? The chance that my only living parent, my mom, could give me, which was unconditional love. There's nothing like a mother's love, right? Mothers are supposed to love their children, right? Take care of their children, right? Why couldn't it have been us against the world, joining forces to become a mother-daughter duo that defied the odds, by turning my dad's death into a positive and not a negative situation? Why couldn't she just love my siblings and me unconditionally? Why couldn't she be happy and thankful that we were her kids? A happy family is all I ever wanted. I wanted to experience her pure, unadulterated love for me. You know, that love that I would never get from my dad because he bailed out on me. I needed her to hold me and tell me how much my dad loved me; how much she loved me. To tell me happy stories about him, about us, about the great man he was and how she loved him and how he loved the both of us. I didn't think it was too much to ask for, yet it was something she was unwilling to give.

As a little girl I was petrified of my mom, but I wasn't the only one. Even some of my family were afraid of her, especially my aunts on my dad's side. Like any normal kid, I would go to my grandparent's home to play and hang out with my cousins. My aunts lived there. I would laugh, talk, get dirty and lose myself being a child. It was one of the places that I was praised for achievement. My aunts used to show off my knowledge of proper words or grown up words. They used to show me off like a trained seal and I don't say that negatively. I remember that they were so surprised that my mom didn't allow me to say the words like "pee pee" or "doo doo". My mom considered that baby talk. Instead my mom expected me to use proper grammar like "urinate" or "defecate or bowel movement". If my mom ever heard me speaking baby talk then I'd catch a whooping. So, going to my grandmother's house was a happy time for me. I didn't have to babysit my siblings when I was at Dears. I loved going to my grandparent's house and playing. I didn't get in trouble or get yelled at like I did at home. I got to be a kid. Everything would be great until it was time for me to go home. The closer her arrival time got, the more everyone felt dread.

The fear was real. All hands were on deck looking under sofas and anywhere they could for the items my mother dropped me off with. What did I do with my clothes? Where were my shoes? Where are my panties? Why didn't I put them all in one place when I got there? All you could hear, from my aunts and me, was alarm for what would happen to me if we couldn't find my stuff. I would get a beat in front of everyone. I had whelps wherever I got hit. I was always cried and melted down. I knew what was going to happen. Everyone felt sorry for me. They felt helpless to stop me from getting beat and cussed out. Those were two inevitabilities if we couldn't find all of my belongings. If I didn't look the exact way, she dropped me off, hell would have no fury like my mom pissed off. I recently asked my Aunt Camille to describe those times, I wanted to confirm if her memories were similar to mine. She laughed and stated that, "It felt like we all would be getting a whipping and yelled at! It wasn't just you your mom affected, Jo, it was all of us. We were terrified for you. We were frantic to save you." Notwithstanding my mom's opinion of me, I was a super obedient child. Dear said that I was her only grandchild she didn't have to spank. For the most part, I never got in trouble anywhere, except for with my mom. I was the ideal child that everyone wanted, except for my mom. I was a burden to her. Why didn't she love me like everyone else loved me?

I knew from my mom, how cruel punishment could be if someone thought you misbehaved; therefore, as I got older, I was the cousin who tried to motivate my other cousins to avoid doing things to get us in trouble. I was the only grandchild that was trusted to drive my grandmother's custom van, yet I got beat for every little thing, by my mom. I got beat with whatever she could grab, a belt, an extension cord, a switch, a shoe, a broom, a whatever.

Dear would always say, "If it doesn't kill you, Sweet Heart, it'll make you stronger." The lingering dysfunctional S.H.I.T! that seemed to plague my life as a little girl, was just a fraction of the things that would help mold me into the fearless woman I am today. One day, I arrived at the conclusion that no matter what I did, it was never going to be enough to make my mother happy. I recall getting my first "B" in the 5th grade. My mother punished me from going outside for the entire summer. I was miserable and inconsolable. I would look out of the window at all the kids playing and just cry. The one thing I loved to do, more than anything in the world, was to go outside and play. I was a tomboy who loved beating all the boys outside, whether it was in dodgeball, kickball, football, Marco Polo, Mother May I, or whatever. I hated having to come in from outside and take a nap. To this day, had I not lived it myself, I would never have believed that something so important to me would be snatched away behind a still-above-average grade of a "B", I mean who does that? My mom.

I already didn't have a childhood, because I was responsible for raising my younger siblings and keeping up the house. My mom struggled financially, so we didn't always have essentials such as food, electricity, water, gas, furniture or a car. Sometimes we had outgrown our clothes but couldn't afford new ones. Sometimes my mom couldn't afford to pay rent so we got evicted a lot. We couldn't afford Christmas sometimes either. We didn't always get toys. We got what we needed; not necessarily what we wanted. We got necessities like panties. Thankfully, my mom's parents, always got us clothes or toys so we did have some good come from Christmas. I was constantly embarrassed. I was terrified that people would know what we didn't have or that my mom would have to borrow money from her parents. Daddy West, would always give, not lend, my mom money when she asked. He often helped us pay rent or buy groceries. She didn't have to pay him back.

I hated it when my mom was desperate enough to borrow money from Mama Harriet. Although she would lend it, she would always rub it in our faces: my mom was too irresponsible to take care of her responsibilities; she shouldn't have had so many kids. To make matters worse, she would tell others about our struggles to people who had no business knowing. Although I'm fast-forwarding, I remember finally having had enough and politely standing up to Mama Harriet, after I got into law school, and begging her to please stop talking about my mother, I was tired of hearing it. I said it as respectfully as I could, but she didn't take it that way, she said I was being disrespectful "talking back"; that since she gave my mom the money, that she was entitled to complain about it. To this day, I don't borrow money because I don't ever want someone to rub it in my face that they did something for me or that I wouldn't be where I am today but for them.

Not only did we have to endure living an impoverished lifestyle, but we had to deal with my mother's codependency on men. No matter what, she had to have a man in her life, even at the expense of treating them better than us, her own kids. For all intents and purposes, because of my mom's codependency, I was the mother of my siblings. Either my mom was working overtime to make ends meet or chasing behind some man. Once she was out with some man and stayed out past midnight. I was babysitting Uchenna as usual. I was in fourth grade and she was three. When my mom finally got home, Uchenna wasn't there. When I'd last seen Uchenna she was asleep in the bed with me. My mom and I were frantic. We had no clue where she was. We went outside searching for her. We ran by the pool hoping she hadn't somehow fallen in and drowned. She wasn't there, thank God.

Just as we passed by the pool, we heard a swing squeaking as it was being pushed. To our surprise, Uchenna was screaming "Weee!", smiling from ear to ear. Some random man was pushing her in the swing in the middle of the night. My mother ran to Uchenna and grabbed her from the swing. I remember her cussing the man who was pushing Uchenna, something to the effect of "why are you pushing a little girl, in a swing, in the middle of the night? Why didn't you try to find out where she lived and get her home?" My mom stormed back to the apartment, carrying Uchenna in one arm and hitting me with the other. She was yelling at both of us. When we got back to the apartment, I got one of the worst beatings of my life. The last time I checked I hadn't given birth to a child, so why in the hell was I held responsible for my baby sister's actions that happened after bedtime when we were both supposed to be asleep, in the middle of the night? For that matter, why were we left at home alone? Hell, I was asleep like I was supposed to be. My mom wasn't home. Why was I being the "responsible party"? Why wasn't my mom responsible for my sister? She was her kid, not mine.

Another time I was watching Uchenna and she got hit by a car. The end of the story is that I got my butt whipped. The beginning of the story was that we, my mom, Uchenna and I were visiting my grandmother in Galena Manor. I wanted to go outside and play with my friends. My mother said I could only go outside if I took Uchenna with me. So, I took her with me. On our way back, Uchenna inexplicably lunged into the path of a car. Fortunately, the only real damage to Uchenna was her feelings. She started crying. I picked her up, tried to stop her from crying, struggled, carrying her back to my grandmother's. I got a beating for that too. Uchenna was two years old then, so I would've been nine.

The dysfunction of my childhood scarred me for a long time. I didn't know how to enjoy my childhood because I had so much adult responsibility. I was constantly under verbal, emotional, and physical attack by my mom. I had to own that my life as an adult didn't have to be like it was as a child. At first, I didn't want children because I was forced to raise my siblings. But then I owned that I didn't have to do things the same as my mom. I didn't have to make my children, if I had any, be responsible for my responsibilities. I could actually give them the freedom to be kids. I had to own that I didn't have to be like my mom if I didn't want to be. I didn't have to beat my kids like my mom beat me. I owned that I had the ability to actually learn from my mom's negative actions towards me.

In fact, when I faced my S.H.I.T! head on, I determined that I would raise my kid the opposite way that my mom raised me. If it hurt me then I wouldn't repeat the pattern with my kids. And most importantly, I knew I had to tell my children that I loved them and that they were a gift from God, daily. I committed that I would never be a lingering chasm of dysfunction for my children. I owned that!

My painful childhood didn't just affect my parenting. It caused me to develop empathy for the pain and suffering of others which probably explains why my law practice and political career have been overwhelmingly dedicated to fighting for the down-trodden with the same fierceness that I fought for my future.

Chapter Four

Suicide as a Family Legacy?

Since my dad killed himself and per my mom, "I was just like my dad", suicide was always an option for me. I was in the 4th or 5th grade, at Foerster Elementary School, when I first tried to commit suicide. I was sick of living such a hard life. Other kids didn't seem to have all of the responsibility that I had. I was tired of getting teased, raising my siblings, and my mom constantly telling me, whenever she was feeling some kind of way, that she "wished I was never born, and I was just like my dad"; that "her life would be so much better without me"; that "she should've aborted me", etc. So, I just wanted to die. I thought if I banged my head hard enough, against a wall, then I would die. I thought wrong. Instead of dying, I had the worst headache. Then I thought taking all of the aspirin in the medicine cabinet would kill me. That didn't work either. There was no suicidal success. I guess I should be thankful now but at the time, I felt like a failure. I couldn't even kill myself right.

I wasn't the only one, in my family, suffering from suicidal ideation, I learned that term from my law practice. Uncle Roscoe admired my dad. He was one of my dad's younger brothers. The night my dad killed himself, Uncle Roscoe told someone that he was going to die just like my dad and ultimately, he did. He shot himself dead, after getting married, having one daughter and serving in the Marines, during Vietnam, just like my father. I was in 9th grade. I never told a soul at Elsik High School. It was our family's secret. Uncle Ravon, another of my dad's younger brothers killed himself too. I learned he killed himself because society didn't give him a chance after he'd served his time in prison and paid his debt to society. He couldn't get a steady job to take care of his two sons, so he figured that if he killed himself then at least the government would take care of his kids. It was summer before my sophomore year in college. I only told one person, outside of my family, about Uncle Ravon's suicide and that's only because he had a huge crush on my college teammate/roommate, Lillian. She knew him and would've noticed his permanent absence. My UH friends or teammates didn't know. My coaches didn't know. I didn't dare tell them. In my world, I was the only person I knew that had experienced suicide. Apart from that, as a Catholic, I didn't want to tell anyone that my family members were going straight to hell. I was ashamed. I didn't want to be different. So it was our family secret. All three, my dad and his two brothers, each shot themselves in the head. Unlike my attempts, their suicides were successful.

My cousin Cassidy tried to kill himself but was unsuccessful. We called him "Lil" Cass because his dad was "Big" Cassidy. Early one Saturday morning, at about 6 a.m., he called me and woke me up. It had better be an emergency calling me that early in the morning, on a weekend. It was. He was crying. He said he was going to kill himself, so he could go be with his mom, Aunt Daphne. She was one of my father's five younger sisters. By way of background, she'd been murdered when we were in high school. I think I was in 12th grade and he was in 11th. She'd been murdered by her pimp. It happened at a crack house. She was shot twice in the head and thrown off of the second floor balcony, in my neighborhood, not three minutes from where I live now. Coincidently, I'd seen the news story about her murder but didn't know it was her. Believe it or not, someone had actually called my grandmother's house and told her that Aunt Daphne was murdered before the authorities actually notified us. Quite naturally my cousins were devastated by their mom's brutal death. He always struggled with her being a prostitute, always getting locked up and being bounced around from family members.

In any case, I begged Lil Cass not to do anything to himself before he spoke with me. I told him I was on my way. He promised he wouldn't harm himself without talking with me first. I threw on some clothes and drove quickly down the street to pick him up. We needed to talk. I called him as I pulled up. He came outside and jumped into my car. He was still crying. I drove us to Frank's Grill to eat breakfast and talk. He was afraid of going to prison. He missed his mom. He told me exactly how he was going to kill himself. Specifically, he said he was going to slit his throat and both of his wrists with his straight razor that he shaved with. He was going to get drunk as hell because it makes the blood thinner and he would bleed out quicker. He was going to do it in the bath tub. He didn't want to make a mess. He explained that the first thing a body does, when it dies, is it expels urine and feces. He'd planned it all out. I was shocked at the level of detail but was thankful that he'd reached out to me.

I begged him not to do it. I told him, to take it from me, as a child of a parent who committed suicide, that he was going to screw his kids up like my dad's suicide screwed me up; that his kids were going to blame themselves for his decision, period, point blank. That they were going to be negatively affected for life. That a part of them would die with him. That they would always wonder "what if". After six or seven hours of talking, he seemed to snap out of his funk. He said he wouldn't do it. I made him promise me on my dad's grave, that he wasn't going to do it. He promised. After our conversation, I was both relieved and thankful that he chose to call me in his time of need and that I was able to help him. I promised him I'd help him and be there for him with whatever problems he was facing.

Early the next Monday or Tuesday morning, as I was getting Jio ready for elementary school, I received a call from Aunt Camille telling me that Lil Cass had killed himself that morning. I was numb and in shock. We'd just talked for hours the Saturday before; and he'd promised me he wouldn't kill himself. Oh my God, I thought I'd talked him out of it. He'd followed his plan to a tee. He'd slit his throat and wrists, while in the tub and was drunk as a skunk. I'm guessing the alcohol gave him the courage to do it. I was beside myself. I didn't take

Jio to school that day. I explained to him that Lil Cass had committed suicide like my dad. Then the next thing I knew, I got a call back saying that he didn't die; that he was being rushed to Ben Taub Hospital. They'd been able to revive him, and it was touch and go. I rushed to the hospital with Jio. After waiting, what seemed like forever, I was told I could go see him. When I got into his room, he was not conscious, but he was alive, thank God. When he finally came to, I was sitting at his bedside. There were only the two of us in the room. I don't remember where Jio was. I wanted to kill Lil Cas, figuratively speaking because he'd scared me to death, but I was sincerely thankful that he was still alive. We talked. We cried. He was so desperate. I just listened.

It sucks, when your family legacy is suicide. It's always stuck in my mind that my grandmother, the one who is most responsible for me not killing myself, lost three sons to suicide. Think about that fact for a moment! No parent should have to bury a child, much less, a child that took his/her own life, yet my grandmother had that cross to bear on three separate occasions! A cross that our Catholic faith taught us led to eternal damnation in hell. My grandmother struggled with that religious teaching for a long time. I know because we discussed it. She didn't want her children to be damned to hell for eternity. No mom wants that for their children.

The cycle of self-murder didn't stop with my father. It started with him. The cycle continued long after he was gone. My family has always tried to explain the tragic events surrounding the untimely suicides of the Jones men, by saying the sins of my grandfather were visited upon his sons. It wasn't just his sons and it wasn't just suicide. It was a curse on his progeny, both boys and girls.

If you truly look closely at my father's side of the family, it appears that the enemy had a contract out against us. Rape, murder, death and destruction followed us. Our reactions to life, whether good or bad, not only affect us as individuals, but it affects those connected to us. The negativity that affected my family was a given but I chose conversely to try and positively influence others. The choice was ultimately up to me. I rebuked that sins of the father philosophy, because if I subscribed to it then I had no choice but to accept the S.H.I.T! that was thrust upon me and my family as a curse, under that scenario, I had no power to stop. I decided that I wasn't going to allow the negative S.H.I.T! in my life to be my WHY?

Why I didn't make it?
Why I didn't live my best life?
Why I didn't live out the purpose I was predestined to live?

After some deep reflection, I realized that this revelation came one day when I was somewhere between 4th and 6th grade. I was in one of my all-time favorite places, outside at the park, in our apartments, Hillcroft Square. It was a hot sunny summer day and kids and families were everywhere around me. Some were in the park, others at the pool, and some were playing on the tennis and basketball courts. When all of a sudden, we all heard screaming. I looked towards the direction of the screaming, through the chain linked fence, and spotted a kid flailing in the water, drowning, going under.

At that moment, it seemed like everything and everyone froze, including me. I grabbed hold of the fence and just watched, as did almost everyone else. There were adults standing around the pool and no one acted; even the mom of the kid who was drowning. She didn't jump in or anything. She was just screaming; frozen in space and place. Out of nowhere a guy, who was playing basketball, ran towards the pool, and dove in, like Superman, and saved that kid from drowning. Clapping and praise erupted. He saved the day like a super hero. I have a specific recollection that I decided that I would never freeze again even during the most traumatic of times. That skill set served me well for the rest of the traumatic events I would face in my life.

I learned a lot from that man's bold and courageous act that saved that child's life, that was destined to end, but for him. Nope, never again I thought. Never again. If it'd been left up to me, that child would've drowned. To me, it didn't matter that I was a child too. When I think about it, I accept that that was a bold decision to make for an elementary school kid, but I did it! That moment spoke to the very core of my being and set off a fire in me that still burns to this day.

Now that I'm older, I correlate my father's death with the pool incident. My dad was that kid that was drowning in his own despair. Those that saw him drowning froze. They didn't know what to do or what to say to help him to save his life. No one knew how to help him or my uncles, for that matter. If ever faced with a life or death situation, I prayed that I would be able to move through the inertia and make things better. That was my expectation for myself. That was me owning my S.H.I.T!

Chapter Five

I Just Wanted You to Love Me

Life was very disrespectful towards me and had no regard for my feelings, my emotions or my potential recovery. At any given moment, life threw me lemons and I had to be strong enough to make lemonade or survive the bitterness.

For the most part, growing up I made straight A's. That fact didn't seem to move my mother at all. I remember getting whippings for earning 97's instead of 100's, which was still an A+. Everyone else, my friends and teammates' parents would dote on me, but my mom never had anything positive to say. Never being good enough was the emptiest feeling ever, because I just wanted her to love me and be proud of me. I needed her approval, as my mother and my only living parent. Deep down within my soul, I loved my mother with every fiber of my being, but I didn't receive the same love in return. The beatings and anger towards me continued well into my teenage years. The fear of my mother was overwhelming. I lived my life walking on egg shells, afraid to make mistakes, of getting beat, or publicly humiliated for her unattainable expectations for me. I never knew from one moment to the next what would set her off; therefore, I was determined to walk the straight and narrow. I had achieved academic success throughout elementary and middle school. I was looking for ways to get away from the home. I was tired of watching my brothers and sisters. I noticed that kids who did sports got to stay at school a little longer, which meant they got home later. So, I started doing sports to have more time not babysitting my siblings. As it turns out, I was really good at running. That was my get away in seventh grade. Sometimes my mom couldn't afford to come get me, after practice, so I got to spend the night over my teammate Falana's house. In eighth grade, I added basketball to my portfolio. I was good at that too. It actually turned out better than I thought because now I had practice before and after school. So now I wasn't just getting home later. I got to leave the home earlier, too. That was great. I was beginning to make a name for myself in sports, plus when we had games or track meets, we got to eat at McDonald's and other restaurants that we couldn't afford with my mom. I was so determined to play sports that I would walk to practice if I had to start in eighth grade. It was dark, and I was walking. I don't know how far it was, but it was far. I didn't care.

When I entered high school, I maintained my academic excellence and became a rising athletic star. I played varsity as a freshman. I was All-State in track and field, having won numerous state titles in the high jump, 800-meters and 400-meters. I'd medaled at State in the long jump. Our 4 x 800-meter relay was ranked in the top 3 in the US. Our 4 x 400-meter relay was state ranked. I had weekly articles written, about me, in the *Houston Post* and *Houston Chronicle*, two local newspapers. I even was named the girl's basketball "Player of the Year", by the *Post* and *Chronicle*, both my junior and senior years. I was All-State in cross-country and was a standout student. I eventually ended up being an All-American in both track and field and basketball. The media always tried to interview me and take pictures at wherever I lived but I always had an excuse why the pictures had to be taken somewhere else. I was getting national recognition but living in total fear that someone would find out that we were living in poverty.

I was ashamed of our living conditions, so much so that I NEVER invited my friends or teammates to whatever rent house or apartment we were living in. I always made up excuses as to why they couldn't come into wherever my family lived but welcomed into theirs. The juxtaposition of how I lived compared to my friends, who didn't have a clue about how I lived, was hard to juggle. They had huge homes, with refrigerators stocked with food and ice cream, the kind of stuff that we might get when my mom got her income tax refund. They had swimming pools, trampolines and late model cars, some of which were convertibles, and way more expensive than any car my mom drove.

I longed for clothes that fit and were up to date. My clothes were old, and my pants were "crabbing", in other words, too short. Some of my teammates teased me regarding my clothes being too small. I was so embarrassed. My mom worked a lot of overtime but it didn't get her from paycheck to paycheck. I decided to find a job. Overtime was my mom's way of life; consequently, she wasn't home a lot. And since she only had one car, I had to find a way to work. That didn't deter me either. Dear always taught me that where there's a will, there's a way.

I was 16 years old and I'd been multitasking for years with raising my siblings, cleaning the rent house or apartment, cooking meals, making good grades and getting to cross country, basketball and track practices, what was one more task. I found my first job working at Bob and Linda's Sandwich shop. It was owned by Jeanie Cain, a lady who my mother delivered mail to. She was a widow. Her husband J.V. Cain had played in the NFL, for the St. Louis Cardinals, he collapsed running routes in practice and died on his 28th birthday. Ms. Cain was so nice and kind to allow me to work for her. I was so excited! I had big plans for my first check. I wanted to buy me a brand-new pair of jeans that weren't crabbing.

After working my first two weeks, it was time for my first paycheck. I thought I was going to get paid cash. That was a currency I understood. Instead I got paid by check. I had no idea how to turn the check into money. I knew nothing about bank accounts or cashing checks. I asked Ms. Cain about cash paydays and she told me to ask my mom to take me to the bank and cash the check for me. Okay, that seemed simple enough, so I asked my mom, when I got home, if she would cash my check for me and give me the cash.

I was expecting a simple, "Ok", but instead she responded with a very vile, "No" and added, "I brought you into this world and I can take you out; any money you earn is mine." She said I didn't have a right to anything. Now, let's pause for a moment, because it is imperative that you understand my pain during this moment. I had worked and labored for two weeks. I was begging for rides to get to work. Still keeping up my grades, the household chores and athletics and my mom took my hard earned money. This was devastating! She took my check and went on like it was nothing. I was crushed! There I was filled with anticipation of finally getting some jeans I could wear; that actually fit me and now this.

Well, life has taught me that most people don't make rational decisions when they are emotionally distraught, and I was no different. I was depressed and feeling sorry for myself. I don't remember how I got to the department store anyway, but I felt that since I worked so hard for my paycheck that I was entitled to those jeans even though my mom took my money. It wasn't fair. There I was in the department store, standing in front of the jeans scared as hell, but willing to take that pair of jeans that my mom denied me.

When I attempted to walk out of the store with the jeans without paying, I got caught. They took me to this room, where they searched me and found the jeans. Then they called the police. I was arrested. I was so embarrassed! At that moment, I realized that even though my mom had done me wrong, by stealing my money, I still had no right to steal from that department store. I knew better. I was raised better. It wasn't fair for me to do to the department store what my mom had done to me. I was in, what I now know as the loss prevention room, only because I'm now a criminal defense lawyer. They held me there until the police arrived. The police came in and handcuffed me.

They then paraded me, aka perp-walked me, out to the police car where they shoved me into the backseat. I had a flood of emotions going through my head, heart, soul and body all at the same time. What had I done? I was a straight A student and star athlete who was in the back of a police car in handcuffs. I was going to be labeled as a thief.

When I sat down in the police car, I leaned over and laid in the seat, for fear that someone would see me. I just knew the whole world was looking directly at me. The cop said, "Sit up and be proud of what you did!" I'll remember those words until the day I die. It's as if it happened yesterday. I'm so lucky it happened when I was a minor because had it happened when I was an adult, I wouldn't have been able to sit for the Texas State Bar exam.

They took me to what appeared to be a jail cell, again, I now know that it was the juvenile holding facility. I remember how cold and dirty it was, with graffiti all over the walls. It smelled horrible, and it was freezing cold. I didn't stay there long and I don't know how the case was resolved. I didn't have to go to court anymore. I'm guessing that some kind of way the case got dismissed. I don't even remember having a lawyer. Regardless, that bad decision that I made taught me one of the greatest life lessons. I decided, that day, I would never take what didn't belong to me, no matter how unfair someone else treated me; that should never be an excuse. I shouldn't make others suffer because of my issues. To reiterate, this was my first real lesson in learning how to own my S.H.I.T!! I was 16 years old!

As sick as this may sound, my mother thrived off my mishaps. She couldn't wait to tell my coach and my grandmother what I had done. She said, "You think Jolanda is so perfect? Well, she's a thief." Yes, my own mother threw me under the bus. She was partially to blame for me flipping out and acting uncharacteristically. Moms are supposed to protect their children but instead, my mom told two people that I respected the most, and who I wanted to respect me, that I was a thief. She used the biggest mistake I'd ever made in my life up until that point, as a weapon against me. Despite my bad choice, I was an honor student and accomplished athlete who'd learned my lesson and who would never make that mistake again. I was a good person who made a bad decision. My mom shouldn't have defined me by the worst thing I'd ever done, at 16 years old.

What mom does that? At that age I didn't fully understand the concept of jealousy, but I felt like my mom hated me and would take any opportunity to destroy me, if she could. "As Jolanda Turns" didn't stop there. One reason I continued to have issues with my mom, I know now, is because my mother refused to change and take ownership of her S.H.I.T!

One day in 11th grade, my mom came home, mad about something as usual. Quite naturally she took it out on me. She went to beat me like she had been doing since I was a kid. Except this day was different. I was sick and tired of getting beat. I don't know why I had the courage on that particular day, at that moment in time, while still living under my mom's roof, where she paid all the bills, but I did.

I'd been taught to never disobey my mom. I mean, hell, she constantly told me that she brought me into this world and she wouldn't hesitate to take me out of it. I believed her. In previous beatings, I just took it. I was so brainwashed that even when I grew taller than my mom in the 8th grade, I still allowed her to beat me and never tried to stop her from doing what she told me she was entitled to do as my parent, the person who brought me into this world and kept me; she didn't give me up or abort me.

With all of this in the back of my mind, she swung the broom at me and, before I knew what I was doing, I had blocked the blow. She wasn't going to finish this beating. Respectfully, I said "No, ma'am, you can't beat me anymore. I'm tired of it. I can't stand it anymore. I won't allow it", or something like that. I was crying and scared. I grabbed the broom. She tried to jerk it out of my hand. She ordered me to let it go because she had the right to finish beating me. Not. It wasn't happening. Not this day. Not by me. She tried to wrestle the broom from me. It was a full-on tug of war. Not! I was stronger than her by now. She was surprised and incensed. I could tell by the look in her eyes. Hell, truthfully, I was surprised, too. I couldn't believe I was standing up to her. I didn't really think about it. It was just reflex.

There I was staring my mom down, with tears in my eyes, defiant, unwilling to allow her to lay her hands, or anything else, on me anymore. She looked up into my eyes, I looked down into hers. When we were wrestling for the broom, in her bedroom, she was yelling that I was a disobedient child and that's what was wrong with me. Truthfully, she always found something wrong with me, which is why I would never and had never lived up to her expectations.

Something inside of me told me this was it, D-Day (Decision Day), the day I decided to control my life when it came to my mom. I just knew I could no longer live under her roof. I didn't know where I would live but I knew it couldn't be there. I didn't trust that I could live there safely. She'd always threatened that she "brought me into this bitch and she would take me out" and I believed her. She then screamed something to the effect of "Oh, what are you going to do now, hit me?" "No, ma'am," I replied respectfully but forcefully, "I'm just not going to allow you to beat me ever again in life." For the record, that was the last time my mom ever beat me! I was 17 years old. Also, to note, my mom had always raised me that a child should never hit their parents. And, in my heart of hearts, I would never, ever hit my mom, ever. She didn't know that, however. I just stared her down. I looked dead into her eyes, hoping that she would see that I was serious. Resolute.

After it was an obvious stalemate, I had to figure out where I was going. I needed an exit strategy. Once I was convinced that if I let the broom go, my mom wouldn't try to hit me again, I let go of it. Without saying a word, I turned and left the house. My mom was screaming at me and demanding to know where I was headed. I told her I was headed to our neighbor's down the street. She told me I didn't have permission to leave the house and I didn't have permission to go to our neighbor's.

Something had changed. I had changed. I was in control of my own life, or so I thought. I would later learn that it takes practice to make good decisions in controlling your own life. In any case, back to D-Day. Uncharacteristically, I defied my mom's orders and continued on to our neighbor's. Our phone service was cut off because my mom couldn't afford to pay the bill but my mom's friend, down the street, had arranged to leave her key hidden outside so that if we ever needed to use the phone, we could use hers.

I marched down the street to our neighbor's, somehow feeling empowered, with my mom yelling down the street for me to come back home, while screaming to whoever would listen that I was a disrespectful and disobedient child. I got the key from its hiding place, unlocked the door, entered the home and called my Dear. I begged her to please come and get me. As I was explaining to her what had just happened, my mom barged in and started screaming to Dear that I was disrespectful and for her not to believe me. She explained all she did was to try and discipline me and I wouldn't let her.

I responded that my mom's version was not true. Oh, why did I say that? My mom lunged at me and tried to take the phone from my hands. Here we go again, we tussled for the phone. She was trying to take it from me and I wouldn't let her. We were both screaming to my grandmother our versions of what was going on. At one point of the tussle; my mom was on my back with her feet dangling in the air. She'd tried to take the phone and I simply turned my body and kept a tight hold on it. Well, she had a tight hold of the phone and my arm and when I pivoted, her body ended up on top of my back.

She screamed for me to let her down and let go of the phone. I told her to just let go of the phone and she would fall back to the ground. Dear told me she was on her way. I was satisfied. I handed my mom the phone and headed back home to pack my stuff, so when Dear arrived, I'd be ready to go. My mom had a few choice words for my grandmother for, in her words, interfering with her ability to discipline her child. I presume she hung up on my grandmother, although I wouldn't know because I'd left. My mom then followed me back to the house yelling and screaming at me but surprisingly, never trying to lay a hand on me.

I think she was afraid that if she tried to hit me again that I would hit her back. Again, I would've never hit my mother, but I'm glad she thought I would because that saved me from having to wrestle or defend myself, with her again. When Dear finally arrived, I put my stuff in her car and we left.

That's the day I moved out of my mom's home. It was the summer before my senior year. I wasn't going back home, so I spent my senior year living with one of my team members and her family. She was two grades younger than me. It wasn't a perfect situation, but it was better than what I was experiencing at home. I was tired of crying all of the time about my mom. My main question was always, why didn't she love me? Dear was so warm and comforting. She knew how to ease me off the cliff of suicide. I thought about it often. Life just seemed like it would never get better. No matter how many awards I won or how great my grades were, my mom was never proud and never pleased with me.

All I ever wanted her to do was to love me. She obviously didn't. I couldn't see, for myself, that it would get better. I couldn't envision a world where my mom was ever proud of me. My grandmother was great at always somehow, some way, convincing me, at the moments in time when I needed it the most, that God didn't make mistakes and that she would be there for me to help figure out how to get through the darkness. I trusted my grandmother and that's why I'm still alive today. Had it not been for Dear, I truly believe that I would've eventually found a way to successfully kill myself since it was always a thought in my mind. I mean hell, my dad did it and he was no longer in pain. Besides that, so many people told me that I was his daughter and I was going to die just like him.

In some ways, I believe that me making a decision to move out of my mom's home, while still in high school was me owning the fact that living in that situation wasn't a healthy environment for me to be in. I recognized that I had to do something to change my situation so that I could have some peace. It was scary. I didn't know where I'd live, when I made the decision to leave, but I knew I could stay at my grandmother's until I could figure it out. I had the rest of the summer to do that.

After my senior year of high school, I was voted the Hertz #1 Award Winner, as the best athlete in Texas, male or female. Interestingly, I was presented the award by OJ Simpson, go figure. I also was the first recipient of the Scholar-Athlete of Houston & Vicinity, for my stellar grades. I graduated Magna Cum Laude. Consequently, I was highly recruited. The big questions were 1) what university I would attend, 2) what sport I would play, basketball, track or both, since I was an all American in both, and 3) would I take an athletic or academic scholarship? I had full scholarship offers from most NCAA Division 1 schools, such as Stanford, USC, UCLA, University of Texas, and its arch rival Texas A&M, TCU, Old Dominion and Tennessee, to name a few. I also had full academic scholarship offers from Harvard, Yale, Dartmouth, Stanford, University of Pennsylvania, Brown, Rice, among others. The Rice University, also known as the Harvard of the South, track coach Victor Lopez, always joked with me that I "was too smart to attend the University of Houston." To this day, I laugh when I think about it. I was being recruited all over the country. The world was my oyster.

To my knowledge, I was literally the first female athlete to have a press conference announcing the college I would attend. Press conferences were generally held only for star male athletes. My first choice was the University of Tennessee, but the track coach left so I finally decided on The University of Houston. The only person who knew my decision before the press conference was my track coach and the UH track coaches. This was the most exciting day of my life. Lights, cameras and reporters were all stationed in one room, anticipating news of what my future would entail. This was my first step to escaping my poverty-stricken and tumultuous life, and I didn't have to pay for anything. I just had to make the big reveal to the world at the press conference.

There I was, the best athlete in Texas, at the hottest press conference in town for male or female athletes. Television and radio stations and print media were everywhere. My mother was nowhere to be seen. I looked out into the crowd, hoping she was running late. I asked if we could hold up and wait for her to get there. For some reason, I thought I needed her next to me. Eventually we had to move forward. I announced my decision, to sign with the University of Houston and that I would accept a track and field scholarship.

When my mom did finally grace us with her presence, she embarrassed the hell out of me by saying she couldn't believe I choose UH over the other schools. When she spoke her mind, I responded by saying that I wanted to "Do what I wanted and not what everybody else wanted". Although my mom's displeasure with my decision wasn't specifically mentioned, the very first sentence, in the story, was a veiled reference to my defense of my decision. I can't begin to express the emotional torment, hurt, pain and embarrassment of my mom's choice to not be supportive of me in public. She stole my thunder that I was entitled to after all the hard work.

Although not on the international level of the Duchess of Sussex, I absolutely identify with her pain and constant betrayal by a parent. I was torn between excitement and fury. I mean she showed up late, she never really supported me, I was living with another family and she couldn't find it in herself to be happy and supportive of me for a couple of hours. If she didn't approve of the school, fine, that was a conversation she and I could've had in private. She didn't have to put our mother/daughter issues on blast to the whole world. I mean, how could outsiders see my value and my worth, yet the woman who carried me for nine freaking months be blind to it? Mere strangers celebrated my accomplishments yet my mother acted as if I hadn't done anything right and, more importantly, that I was and always would make bad decisions.

I had tried my whole life to do something, whether it was excelling academically, athletically, joining organizations, or whatever, to accomplish something so she'd love me, be proud of me, and be happy with my success. To make her see that my father's death, although tragic and life altering, wasn't in vain, because he lived on in, and through, me. I was so focused on proving something to her that I almost lost myself.

Hoping for the best with my mom always led to disappointment and heartbreak, so I began to lower my expectations. I was beginning to learn that if I had no expectations then I was less likely to be disappointed. Unfortunately, lowering my expectations was easier said than done.

Chapter Six

A Taste of Racial Reality

After leaving my mothers' home, I was convinced that all the crazy S.H.I.T! was over. I was in control. No more beatings. No more living in fear while feeling inferior. No more struggling. I could finally breathe, or so I thought. I had to figure out where I was going to live for my senior year. My grandmother lived in Third Ward. I'd lived in Alief, since 8th grade and was heading into my senior year at Elsik. I didn't want to switch schools in 12th grade.

I called a friend and track teammate and her mom; and they allowed me to move in with them for my senior year. My mom didn't approve and wanted me to move back home but I wasn't going to take anymore beatings and she wasn't prepared to change. Truthfully, after moving out of my mom's home, it was the first time that I didn't have grown up responsibilities.

Even though I missed my younger brothers and sisters, I felt relief, not having to raise them. I hate to say it, but I was glad I wasn't responsible for taking care of them anymore and running a household. I later found out that my siblings were really sad when I left. I wasn't able to speak to them much because my mom was mad about me leaving. I also wasn't allowed to call or come by.

Moving in with my teammate seemed like a wonderful idea and a dream come true. Anything was better than staying with my mother. The family was Anglo. They were very generous for allowing me to live with them. The mother sold jewelry and the father was a private investigator. They were self-employed. I grew up in a home where my mom had to work overtime to make ends meet. This family owned their own businesses. They weren't scraping around for money. Their life was nothing like mine. They owned, not rented, a nice home. They had nice cars. Everyone in the family, except my teammate's younger sister, owned a car. Even my teammate, who was two years younger than me, had her own car, a two-toned blue and silver convertible. I can't remember the model, but I think it was something like a Mazda RX7 or Corvette. In any case, it was a late model 2-seater convertible. Are you kidding me? She was in 10th grade. She had a better car than my mom. There was always food. The kids were given allowances. What, huh? Allowances? Hell, we didn't have enough money to last from paycheck to paycheck, much less extra money to give to anyone, especially a kid. My mom took the money I actually earned from working.

We never had extra money, ever. Well, maybe my mom had extra money, for herself, during income tax time when she got her refund. The family I lived with were so much nicer than my mom. Unlike my mother who lived by the "do or die" tactic: You do what I say or die. This family actually gave their children choices. My siblings and I had better be grateful for the roof over our head, the little food we had and the clothes on our backs that my mom provided. I never heard my teammate's mom or dad rub in their children's faces that they were a burden. I never heard constant complaining by their parents. They weren't in any danger of being evicted or having the lights or water turned off. They had a refrigerator full of food, at all times, not just when they got paid. In fact, I don't recall them getting paid every two weeks like my mom. Money didn't appear to be a problem. Their world didn't seem to revolve around money and if there was enough of it or what bills would or wouldn't be paid monthly. Since I was a guest in their home, I got an allowance too. Wow, that was the first time I actually had extra money. My point is that I got a chance to see just how green the grass could be on the other side. Pools, trampolines, cars, allowances and no constant nagging and getting beat by your mom. The grass was green, but my life was still dark. I missed my siblings. I was tired of trying to explain why I didn't live with my family. I was tired of being harassed by my mom for living with an Anglo family.

Witnessing my teammate and her sister with their parents was somewhat sad because I didn't have that opportunity to have a loving relationship with my mom. I would never know the security and warmth of being cuddled by both of my parents. Nor would I ever see them in a room together interacting or cheering for me, in excitement, at a track meet, basketball game or awards ceremony. This was very difficult, but I was determined not to go back to the same old S.H.I.T! Even though I saw what I didn't have, it was better because that experience enabled me to see how I could live when I grew up if I just stayed focused.

Although there was no overt racism in the house, there was an incident that took place that should've warned me of their true feelings regarding race. I was too young and naïve to understand. I went to church with their family, every Sunday. One day at church, a congregant made an announcement about a mission work she'd done. From the pulpit, she shared, with not a lick of hesitation and from her heart, that she and some others had "helped a nigger child… at a camp for the poor." What? I was stunned! It was the first time in my life that I felt "Black" and it wasn't a nice feeling.

Prior to that, I'd looked at the world as color blind. In my naïve world, we were all created equal and we all saw each other that way. It was the first time I saw two separate worlds. I immediately looked around the church and realized that I was the only Black person present. I also realized that everyone had turned to look at me. I tried so hard to be invisible. I felt so embarrassed; so awkward. I didn't know what to do or say. I felt hurt. I actually wanted them to get up and that we all leave but that didn't happen.

We just continued to sit and listened to the remainder of the service like nothing inappropriate was said or done. I couldn't focus on anything anyone said after that. I couldn't understand why the family didn't say anything. It was obvious to me that this "nigger" word occurrence was normal. I'd heard about racism from my mom. How she had been called a nigger; and how the Ku Kux Klan burned a cross at her parents' home when she was a little girl. Their neighborhood was Galena Manor, which was near Pasadena, where a local branch of the KKK was based. Interestingly, I had seen bill boards advertising the grand-dragon or cyclops or something of the KKK every time the Elsik track team drove to San Jacinto Junior College for the regional track meet; every year for four years.

For whatever reason I was under the impression that even though those bill boards were up in Pasadena, I figured that they were old and that racism really didn't exist, but if it did, then is way over in Pasadena. Geographically, Pasadena was far from Alief so if racists did exist, then they mostly lived in Pasadena. I had never actually heard the word "nigger" used in a public space, especially at church, by an adult. I thought that happened a long time ago in some far away land, not now and with me in the room with it. At that moment, I saw and felt my Blackness, and by the looks of everyone staring at me, they knew I was Black too.

Interestingly, I hadn't appreciated that I was Black in terms of being different from them being White. Well, that reality was shattered! All I'd seen was a nice family who became my saving grace during a time when I needed to be rescued, from my home life. It had never occurred to me that I was a charity case. My relationship with the family changed that day. I felt weird still living there when I knew they thought it was okay to call us "niggers."

When we returned from church, I brought up the use of the word "nigger". I just couldn't understand why it was necessary to describe that poor child as a "nigger child". Why did his color even matter? I felt uncomfortable saying the word, why hadn't they said anything? The mom tried to explain away the use of the word "nigger" by trying to convince me that it wasn't meant in a derogatory way. I didn't buy her explanation, but I understood that it wouldn't pay off to argue about it, so I just shut up. I began planning my exit strategy. I was so close yet so far from being on my own. I was in 12th grade and was planning to attend the University of Houston on a full scholarship. If I could just make it to the fall, I would soon be living in the dorm all on my own.

What was so surprising to me was that this family, who had taken in a Black child, me, was okay with the word "nigger" and that they believed that the negative connotation of the word "nigger" could be explained away. My brain was reeling. I was trying to figure out how I missed that this family either supported or acquiesced to a racist mentality.

I started looking back to see what else I had either missed of overlooked that showed that racism existed in my world, in Alief. I flashed back to my freshman year at Elsik. The traditional freshman fundraiser that raised money for our senior prom was the "Slave Sale". Freshman were auctioned off to more senior students. I felt uncomfortable with the whole notion of auctioning off anyone as a slave, but I wrote it off to kids not understanding political correctness. They weren't Black, and they didn't understand what the true history of the slave trade was to Africans, and ultimately African Americans. Plus, Black freshman participated in the fundraiser too. I wanted to fit in and didn't have the courage to say anything about it. I wanted to do my part to raise money for our senior class to offset the cost of prom. So, I'd decided to participate. A white classmate of mine was auctioned with me. We were sold as a pair. I don't remember how we got paired together but what was extra bad, about our sale, was that we were the only slaves sold who were actually made to dress like "African cannibal slaves". If my memory serves me correctly, we were auctioned off for a mere $5 dollars, when all other slaves were auctioned off, a single person purchases, for more than four times what the two of us were sold for. I think the highest auctioned off freshman, went for more than $50 dollars. I was embarrassed because we went for so cheap. That cheap price was meant as a direct shot at me because I had played varsity basketball, as a freshman, and my teammates didn't like it. No freshman, much less a Black girl, had ever played varsity as a freshman.

I was ostracized on our team by some of my

teammates. On team trips, I sat at the front of the bus with my coach, rather than sitting in the back where I'd be bullied, to and from games. Back to the slave sale, my classmate had the misfortune of being sold with me, so she had to dress like a cannibal too. They had us wear bikini tops (white and red striped), grass skirts, with bones tied into our hair. A picture of us, was placed in the yearbook that year, to be memorialized forever. It was obvious that they wanted to demean me. I wanted to cry but I didn't. I put on a happy face as if I was in on the joke but looking back, that was racist. There were more examples that I won't go into but needless to say, I was too young and naïve to appreciate the racism of it. I didn't look at the totality of circumstances. I couldn't see the forest for the trees.

My "nigger child" experience taught me to value myself as an individual. It also forced me to try to figure out ways to extricate myself from those types of situations. I'd already been beaten down by life and I wasn't about to allow an epidemic that's been going on for centuries – racism - to stop my trajectory out of poverty. I didn't care that they called a poor needy Black child a nigger. I was NOT a nigger! I was an upwardly mobile young person. I was an athletic and academic superstar, student leader and tutor. I was created equal, even if they didn't accept it.

Prior to me moving with that Anglo family, my mother had a major issue with me living in a fairytale world where race didn't matter. She kept trying to warn me, to prepare me for the inevitability that, regardless of my belief that we should be judged by the content of our character and not the color of our skin, someone was going to remind me, of the exact opposite, that race did matter. Being a great person or great athlete or great student didn't alter the inevitable, yet sad, truth that race mattered to some.

I would always be Black. As much as I didn't want my mom to be right, she was exactly right. Once I learned that lesson, I was able to adjust. It hurt profusely to be blind-sided by something I didn't believe existed and wasn't prepared for.

But, now that I understood that some people, regardless of merit, believed they were just better than me, I would be prepared moving forward.

Although racism was now on my radar, I would use their supportive family dynamic, to help be a road map for success. I compared what I learned from them to what I saw on the Cosby Show. A Black male physician and a Black woman lawyer who were married, had nice things, living in a nice home, with four Black children. They were able to take ugly life lessons and create humorous teachable moments, causing everyone to love them along the way. I now had a blueprint for success and I was determined to put the pieces together, brick by brick, while rising to the top. Being rich would solve all of my problems from poverty to racism.

College was my first step to riches and the easy life. I'd have my own place for the first time in my life. I'd be in control of my destiny with the gifts God gave to me. Dear had helped me to reach that understanding. She said that I could do anything I put my mind to. My S.H.I.T!, unbeknownst to me, was shaping my resolve. It was showing me that no matter what hit me or how hard it hit, that I could survive. I was becoming like tungsten.

The day of high school graduation finally arrived and as I walked across the stage to receive my diploma, I made a conscious effort to leave the trauma of my S.H.I.T!, in the rearview mirror. The next phase of my life began as I exited the stage, with diploma in hand. I did it! I made it, and no one could take that away from me! Interestingly, I didn't want to participate in graduation, I just wanted my diploma, but my mom made me participate anyway. In my mind, this was the last time I had to do something my mom made me do.

I had every possible excuse in the book to allow for my failure, if I chose to accept them; to believe them, to use them; or to rely on them. But something inside me constantly told me that there had to be a better way to live when I grew up. I wasn't going to live as an adult like I was forced to live as a child. I just wasn't going to let this happen to me! I was going to figure out how to change my trajectory. I was going to control my future and my life; I was going to ask questions; pay attention; fight through whatever! I had to run and jump hurdles with my game face on despite the pain. I had to work hard to not take my dad's way out through suicide. I'm just thankful that I was smart enough to reach out for help to people in my life I trusted.

Whether I knew it or not, the best thing I could've ever done for me, was asking for help. It wasn't a sign of weakness but just the opposite, it was a show of strength. I had to make my S.H.I.T! be the fuel that drove me to succeed in athletics and in school rather than to allow it to bury me in its stench. Rather than allow my mother's deeply imbedded hardships to make me feel worthless and unworthy of love, I made it my fuel to drive me to succeed in life, because I didn't want to repeat her cycles of misery. I didn't want to be my mother. Thankfully, Dear taught me that no one is all good and no one is all evil. In the best people there's some bad, and in the worst people, there's some good. In other words, just as we are not the best thing we've ever done, conversely, we're not the worst thing we've ever done. So I tried to find positive lessons from some of the negative lessons I learned from my mom.

Despite the S.H.I.T!, my mom's, my dad's, mine, I graduated. I took all the negatives and somehow…someway; I created positives. The operative words were "somehow" and "someway" and "created." I had to put in some work. The somehow and someway didn't just fall out of the sky. I had to learn not to take S.H.I.T! personal, nor permanent! When one path to success didn't work, I had to step back and look for a path forward, through a fresh pair of eyes and an uncluttered mind. I didn't have any more excuses and I wasn't about to use my trauma as a crutch to hang around the hood and not excel.

I didn't have to answer to my mother anymore. I didn't have to live with my teammate anymore. I didn't have to struggle, or so I thought, because now I was free to be me and make my own way. I was going to enjoy the process of finally coming into my own truth and my own identity. I was college bound and life was about to become a grand successful adventure. I'   d been faking an ideal life on the outside until I made it! My plans were to graduate from college and to make the United States Olympic team, win multiple gold medals and become a successful lawyer. Nothing was going to stand in my way. I was the "determiner" of my fate. Unbeknownst to me, life was going to continue to shower me with tsunami waves. Was I prepared? Would I be able to swim to shore? Could I hold my breath? I was about to learn to sink or swim.

Suffering Hardship Internalizing Trauma

Chapter Seven

College Didn't Save Me

The time had finally come for me to move into my dorm and I was extremely excited about this new life I was about to embark upon. I was ready to meet new people. I could now come and go as I pleased. I didn't have someone hovering over me with demands and micromanaging my time and activities. I relied heavily on my favorite aunt, Camille. She warned me that boys could be dangerous to my life's future plans. I had a grown up decision to make. She told me that I needed to get on birth control pill. I didn't want to because I wasn't having sex and didn't plan on it until I was married. I didn't even have a boyfriend. She said that boys can make you do things you don't want to do or that you think you won't do. I was strong-willed and didn't believe a boy could make me do anything.

Aunt Camille finally convinced me to get on the pill just to be safe. She took me to Planned Parenthood. When we arrived, protesters were there accusing everyone of getting abortions and being baby killers. They had posters up of dead and bloodied fetuses. I wasn't even having sex yet they were accusing me of being pregnant. We didn't end up going through the gauntlet of protesters. To say that I was traumatized was an understatement. All I wanted was to get birth control pills but instead we left empty handed. That's why I'm such a supporter of Planned Parenthood to this day. My aunt only wanted to take me there for pregnancy prevention. My aunt took me to another place but we couldn't afford them, so we returned to Planned Parenthood, where birth control was affordable. It was based on income and I had no income. My aunt had to give me a pep talk before entering the gauntlet. The mob of protesters tried to block our entry, but we got through. I got my birth control and prepared to begin college.

I certainly didn't expect for boys to side track me. A full-ride scholarship meant I would no longer have to worry about money and therefore I could focus. I knew my goals and intended to achieve them. All I had to do was get to college.

I had never had a boyfriend in high school. I'd gone to prom with my best friend, Troy Bearden, because he felt sorry for me. The boy I liked didn't like me back. I had vented to Troy how no one asked me to prom. We were at a track meet in Aldine. He was shy and was afraid to ask the girl he liked to prom, so he said, "we should just go to prom together!" I was like, "really". He said, "yeah!" Done deal, prom dates we were. The girl he liked eventually asked him to prom, but he'd already asked me. Prom was uneventful. We didn't have that good a time because almost everyone was with their girlfriend or boyfriend and we were just friends. Everyone, except Troy and I, went to hotel after-parties later. We just went home. Prom was a big disappointment. Boys had never been a distraction to me. I had no experience with them. I had no idea the trouble boys could lead you into. Aunt Camille's words would be prophetic for me for years to come.

During my freshman year I started dating a childhood friend who'd like me for a long time. Things were going well, or so I thought. I wanted to save sex for when we got married. He said that was okay at first but then he started pressuring me to have sex. I spoke to Aunt Camille, who was my favorite aunt, about it. I held out for a long time but then Aunt Camille said that if I didn't have sex with him then some other girl would. I was sure I was going to lose him. Then Aunt Camille suggested that I arrange to take him to meet another girl until I was ready to have sex with him. As crazy as it sounds, I used to drive him to the girl's house, which was over by Peck Elementary. Aunt Camille allowed me to use her car to take him over there. She told me so long as the girl didn't live in Third Ward, no one would know he was sleeping with someone other than me. I was concerned that people would think he was cheating on me. I didn't think they would understand how or why I would take him to hook up with another girl. Hell, I really couldn't understand it myself but Aunt Camille had convinced me that this was the right thing to do. My feelings were still hurt that he wouldn't wait on marriage for me but I was more afraid to lose him. The thought of him touching another girl was driving me crazy. After a period of time, I couldn't take it anymore so I gave in and had sex with him. It was the only way I knew to stop him from being with the other girl and to just be with me. That was our agreement.

That first time we had sex lasted all of one minute for him before he climaxed. Then it was over. I felt nothing but the pain of him trying to enter me. No climax. No nothing. To say that I was disappointed was an understatement. I'd heard so much about sex and how great it was supposed to feel. Then he asked me how it was for me and I lied and told him it felt good. He seemed so excited about finally sleeping with me. To make matters worse, notwithstanding me being on the pill, I got pregnant. That was the last thing I expected. Here I was, a star athlete on a full scholarship, about to lose it all over a one-sided minute of ecstasy and an unplanned pregnancy. Having a baby was permanent. I already knew how hard it was to care for kids. I knew having a child would affect my plans. I had to make a decision and I had to make one quick. I'd just got a scholarship and I wasn't ready to lose it. I spoke with my boyfriend about the predicament we found ourselves in. He was a senior in high school. I was just a freshman in college. He wasn't ready for kids and neither was I. After careful consideration, we chose to have an abortion. I couldn't afford to raise a baby and I refused to bring a child into the world to live in poverty. On a side note, it turns out that the girl I was taking him to meet with wasn't the only girl he was sleeping with. Unbeknownst to me, he was cheating on me with this other girl, who I later found out he had two kids with.

I still had a nagging need to have a close relationship with my mom. I was hopeful that we might have a better relationship since I no longer was a financial burden on her. Apart from that, I wanted an assurance that my boyfriend and I had made the right decision related to the abortion. I reached out to my mom and confided in her about the abortion. I wanted an unbiased opinion. It was the most serious decision I'd made in my young life. I was trying to save my future as I'd envisioned it. I spoke with my mom about it. She told my grandmother. It went something like this: Oh, you think Jolanda's so perfect, well she's not. She had an abortion. We were Catholic and abortion was considered a sin. I was devastated in her betrayal of me. To my chagrin, nothing had changed since high school. I felt in my heart that she should've taken my secret to the grave with her. Mother's shouldn't use their children's weaknesses or mistakes against them.

I didn't know how to face my grandmother. I didn't know what to say to her about what my mom told her about me. I didn't want her to be disappointed in me. As it turned out, my grandmother told me that she loved me despite what my mom said. She didn't judge me. And most surprisingly, she never asked if it was true or not. Why couldn't my mom be like my grand mom? Me wanting us to have a close relationship obviously wasn't enough to make us have a close relationship. For now, I just had to be careful with what information I shared with my mom because I knew that if she felt like getting back at me, she would definitely use sensitive information against me. Unlike my mom, I knew I could always trust and rely on my grandmother.

College was more challenging that I envisioned. Rather than it being the nice place I thought it would be, it was full of traps that I hadn't anticipated. I thought that since I was a responsible kid, an A-student, world class athlete, hard worker and self-starter, that I would fit right in, in college. I had no idea how much I would need my grandmother's unconditional love and support as an adult. I thought I could rely on myself. Stupid S.H.I.T! continued to happen. I was so used to wearing shame as a trench coat that it wasn't so easily taken off in.

I was always overly concerned about what people thought of me and I hated to get in trouble for anything. I would sit at the front of the class to ensure I was in plain sight of the teacher, so I could see the board and hear the lectures, I didn't miss class and I took meticulous notes because it was important for me to make the highest grade in class. My focus on academics paid off. I had a high GPA. A number of semesters I had a 4.0 GPA. My roommate had a C average. I took 10 – 15 pages of notes in all of my classes, plus I had perfect attendance. When it was test time, I would just study my class notes in preparation. To my knowledge, she didn't take meticulous notes like me. She would study her text books in test preparation. I'd make A's. She'd make C's. For whatever reason, she thought she should make A's. She didn't. So she started a rumor that I cheated. I graduated from college with a 3.73 GPA. You don't cheat your way to that GPA. I'd always worked my butt off and to maintain good grades my whole life. Now I was falsely being accused of cheating and some people actually believed it.

I was finally away from my mother and her always accusing me of things I didn't do and now this. I'd always prided myself in my grades. I was hurt and distraught about the lies my roommate started about me. I went to my grandmother's crying. I explained what happened. Dear asked me if I cheated. I answered, "no, ma'am". She asked me, "then why are you crying?" I explained that people were believing lies about me and that I had actually worked hard for an A+ average. She reminded me that Jesus lived for 33 years on this earth. Before he was born, the powers that be tried to kill him. After he was born, he was forced to live amongst the leapers and prostitutes, and others that society looked down upon. While he was healing the sick and poor and blessing humanity, he was betrayed by Judas, his disciple, and then they killed him. Yet Jesus didn't do anything to anybody and he was without sin. She continued, "Sweet heart, why do you expect to be treated better than Jesus Christ?" I thought about it and thought, maybe she has a point. She said his parents knew he was destined for greatness. They had to make sure he was born so they slept in a barn with animals. They weren't comfortable. Once born, they had to keep him safe. When he became a man, he fought to stay alive until he was betrayed by those close to him. And even after the betrayal, he still died to save us. He had to fulfill his purpose and I had to fulfill mine.

She then went on to explain that even when I make a mistake, if people make fun of me, then I need to look at it like I looked at a pencil. So, she held up a pencil, and repeatedly asked me what I saw. I repeatedly answered, "a pencil." Each time I gave that answer, her response was, "Wrong answer." I was trying to figure out how this discussion about people falsely accusing me of cheating had turned into her asking me what a pencil was. I didn't see the relevance. I was also irritated because it seemed like she was wasting my time. I needed her to console me and tell me those people were wrong. I needed her to help me figure out a way to convince my "friends" that I did NOT cheat and have them believe me and stop spreading rumors. She wasn't doing what I went there for her to do. She continued, "The obvious answer is that it's a pencil, but the obvious is not always the answer, you must look deeper." After still not getting the point, she finally said, "The right answer is that pencils are more than pencils. Pencils have erasers attached to them, so they are as one. If we were perfect, pencils wouldn't need erasers." In other words, people make mistakes. When a mistake is made, the mistakes should be evaluated. The mistakes shouldn't be allowed to destroy you. The point is, you can erase the bad; and even though remnants of what you erased might remain, you can always write over it by doing something different." All of a sudden, I got it. I wiped my tears and my nose. I realized that the haters were going to keep on hating and that there was probably nothing that I could do about it but so long as I knew I was innocent of their accusations then I should keep surviving and do what I needed to do to continue on to greatness despite them. And if somehow I faltered, then I just needed to reflect on the mistake, erase that behavior, and do better the next time.

Christmas Break of my freshman year was not happy. Although I was on a full scholarship, unbeknownst to me, a full-ride didn't provide housing during the Christmas holidays so I had to move out of the dorms. With nowhere else to go, I went to stay with my mom. Although I didn't realize I would ever have live with my mom again, a bright spot was that I would get to see my siblings. I missed them because I really hadn't seen or talked to them since I'd moved out the summer after 11th grade, which was a year and a half prior. Greg had gotten out of jail recently and was living with mom. Even though Greg and my mom had dated on and off for years, I never accepted him as my stepfather. Here's one reason why. It involved my baby sister. Greg was mad at my sister for something. He was yelling at her. The next thing I knew, Greg had literally picked India up and thrown her against the wall outside of the bedroom. She was crying. I picked her up off of the floor and made sure she was okay. I comforted her as best as I could. After I made sure she was okay, I went to my mom's room and asked to speak with her alone since she and Greg were now laying in the bed. My mom said she wasn't moving and that Greg didn't have to leave her room. She said that whatever I said to her I could say in front of Greg. I explained that Greg had just thrown India against the wall and that his actions were child abuse and that she needed to do something about it. India was seven years old, I was 19. My mom responded that Greg's actions were not child abuse. She said that Greg had already told her what happened; that India had done something she wasn't supposed to do and he'd only disciplined her. I argued to the contrary and told her that if he laid his hands on my sister again that I would call the police. I wasn't in love with him and distracted like she was. I then went back into the room with India and tried to make her feel better. The next thing I know, my mom came into the room where I was, grabbed my belongings, and began to throw them onto the front lawn. She told me that I had to get out now. She said that Greg told her that my actions were unacceptable. He said he was the man of the house and he couldn't have a child being disrespectful to him.

He gave her an ultimatum; either I went, or he went. My mom chose him. My heart was broken. The next thing you know, I was out on the front lawn with my belongings, crying my eyes out. Yet again, I had to find a way to leave my mom's house. This time, I called the family I'd stayed with my senior year in high school and asked them if they could come and pick me up and take me to my grand mom's house, which was in Third Ward. I was devastated that my mom picked her man over me but, honestly, she always treated her men better than she treated us. I felt such rejection. I was also embarrassed to have to explain my situation to the Anglo family.

My mom had locked me out of the house. I had to pick my clothes up from across the yard. I didn't have a suitcase or anything. I'd just gathered them all in my arms. My siblings saw all of this. They weren't allowed to speak to me or come outside with me. All of the neighbors could see me. It was humiliating, and I was worried about India getting in trouble since I chose to stand up for her. I realized that they still needed protection and I couldn't do anything about it. I felt helpless. When was my mom ever going to pick me? When was she ever going to love me? I was inconsolable. When was I ever going to have a happy life with a loving family? Why was I not good enough to have my only living parent love me?

When the family came and picked me up, I got in their SUV. I couldn't stop crying. I told them where my grandmother lived, and we headed there. The mom, dad, my teammate, her sister and their grandmother were in the SUV. The mom was trying any and everything to make me stop crying. She asked me how Christmas was. I think she was trying to distract me. Her question actually did take my mind off of my dilemma. I told her that Christmas was good. I explained that I was proud to have been able to get my siblings what they wanted, for Christmas, instead of what they needed. I'd saved my meal money and the good-grade-money I'd earned from Aunt Camille. Uchenna was 13 years old. She wanted a Swatch, which was a popular brand of watch, and I was able to buy her one. Chuck wanted walkie talkies. He was eight years old. I bought him a set. My brother Ulmer wanted Teenage Mutant Ninja Turtle action figures. He was three years old. I bought him them. I lamented that the only sibling I didn't get what she wanted was India. She wanted a Hart Family doll set, which consisted of a mom, dad and daughter. What was unique about the Hart Family was that they sold them in different races. I tried to find a Black Hart Family, but I couldn't find any. All I could find were White ones, so I ended up buying India a tea cup set. India was a little sad because she'd had her heart set on a Hart Family. The Anglo mom asked me why I didn't just buy her a White Hart Family? I explained that my mom didn't allow us to play with White dolls. My mom always said White people don't play with Black dolls so Black people shouldn't play with White dolls. In response, the Anglo mom said passionately, "that's not true, I had a nigger doll when I was a child?" I was shocked. I almost fell out. All of a sudden, I felt Black, in a car full of White people. It took me back to when we were in church and that lady had referred to helping that 'nigger child'." I felt super awkward and couldn't wait to get to my grandmother's house, but we were on the Southwest Freeway, by the Malibu Grand Prix, where the people were murdered, and my grandmother's house was still far away. I was speechless and didn't say anything else. I didn't know what to say and I felt uncomfortable being in their car. I was trying to figure out how they were racist but let me stay with them my senior year, and they were taking me all the way to Third Ward. It didn't make sense to me. They kept talking but I didn't really hear them after that. I was so disappointed. I just wanted to get to my grandmother's as fast as we could.

When we got to my grandmother's neighborhood, there were wooden "shot gun" houses. They got their name from the fact that they were so small that you could shoot a shot gun and the bullet would travel from the front door and out the back door. They were mainly found in poor neighborhoods. There were convenience stores, people hanging out in the neighborhood and people drinking. The area was not well maintained because the city historically neglected my neighborhood. Out of nowhere, Ally, my former teammate's younger sister, she was in 9th grade, stated, "man

Jo, I knew you came from a neighborhood like this." Her facial expression told it all. Clearly it wasn't a desirable neighborhood and definitely not the type of neighborhood her family would ever live in. Wow, that was strike two. Her mom's "nigger doll" comment was strike one. Again, I didn't know what to say, so I remained silent. When we finally drove up to the back of my grandparent's property, the dad said, "Jo, who do all of these cars belong to?" I was stunned. He was shocked that there were a number of nice cars on the property. I answered, "The Audi is my aunt's. The custom van is my grandmother's. And, the three Cadillacs are my grandfather's." I went on to explain that my aunt was a double engineering major from Prairie View A&M and that she worked for a big oil company, as an engineer. She made a nice salary. She was the one who put braces on my teeth and gave me $20 for A's and $10 for B's. She bought the Audi for herself and the custom van for her mom, my grandmother. My grandfather owned a body shop and when people didn't pay their bill, he got to keep their cars. He loved Black Cadillacs. They were legally my family's. The dad's comment was strike three. After I got out of the truck, I thanked them for the ride and never spoke to them again.

At some point I realized that people can be racist and still "help" those that they feel superior to. To a certain extent, their interaction with me was like the "White Man's Burden...," Rudyard Kipling's poem, about colonial control of a people. In other words, it's like Eurocentric racism and American imperialism. It's the notion that White people are superior people and must save the rest of the world and inferior civilizations. Think Tarzan and the animal-like Africans or the British and their treatment of the aboriginals. I was disappointed in that family, but it taught me a lot. I prefer in-your-face racists because at least I know who they are. The scarier racists are those who don't believe they're racists. I had to own that all that glitters ain't gold and the grass isn't always greener.

I ran into my grandparent's house and cried, not only about my mom picking a man over me, but also, a confirmation that a family that I believed saw me as equal, actually believed me to be inferior and needing them to save me. That Christmas was one of the most disappointing Christmases I ever had. I couldn't wait for the Spring semester to start. To get back to achieving my goals through education. I had to stay focused. I was learning that life didn't get easy just because I was in college.

Suffering Hardship Internalizing Trauma

Chapter Eight
Loving From A Distance

My mom finally got a job at the post office right before Uchenna was born. She was a letter carrier. She looked so forward to having a government job with good benefits. I was six years old. I remember her having high hopes. Those hopes were dashed pretty quickly. Almost immediately, my mother hated her job with a passion. She always came home tense, angry, exhausted and full of anxiety. Basically, just always in a bad mood. She had to work a lot of overtime to make ends meet. A few bright spots in her very dark world were some of the nice people on her route that she delivered mail to. But those postal supervisors were a piece of work; they lived to exert undue influence on carriers. That's why she joined the union and eventually became a union steward; to help stave off supervisors who were too busy accusing carriers of crimes they didn't commit, in order to get them fired or dock their pay or put them off of the clock. It's interesting that I recognized the value of unions at such a young age. To this day, I consider myself a union girl.

Almost every day, my mom came home complaining about her job to me. One particular story sticks in my mind. I was in elementary school. She had just returned to work from maternity leave and she was bleeding heavily. She went to the restroom to change her sanitary napkin and the supervisor accused her of faking having to go to the restroom rather than sorting the mail for her route and getting out to deliver it. He publicly berated her, in the presence of her co-workers, and wrote her up. To defend herself, she marched back to the restroom, grabbed her bloody sanitary napkin out of the trash and took it and placed it on her supervisor's desk to prove she wasn't slacking or lying. He fronted her in public. She defended herself in public. She couldn't believe it and vented to me. I heard these stories when my mom came home almost every day. It seems like she was forced to file grievances to earn any semblance of dignity at work. I never looked forward to her coming home from work, because I knew it was going to be some S.H.I.T!! Her mood was so bad that I decided, at an early age, that I wasn't going to work at a job that I hated because miserable moms make miserable kids.

So, when she came home, if everything wasn't in order then I would get beat. When Uchenna was just a baby, less than a year old, she was crying and wouldn't stop. My mom spanked her. After that, every time Uchenna cried, I tried, as fast as I could, to try and get her to stop crying because I didn't want her to catch a whooping. If I couldn't get her to stop crying, I knew my mom was going to whoop her, so I would offer to take her whooping for her. I tried really hard to protect my siblings. No kid should have to do that, but I felt like I needed to.

My mom was always cruel in her discipline of me. I remember one time she said I did something, I don't remember what it was, but I do remember this particular beating. She made me lay on the bed, on my stomach. I was supposed to lay there while she beat me. Whenever the belt was about to land on my skin somewhere, I moved to try and blunt the blow. She kept screaming for me to lay still but my self-preservation instinct kicked in and wouldn't allow me to just lay there and get beat. The next thing I know, my mom made me get naked, then she made me get in the tub, she ran water on me to get me wet. I think it was done for the express purpose to make the licks sting more for punishment for not laying still when she beat me. Then she tied me to the baby bed since I wouldn't lay still. Then she proceeded to beat me until I couldn't even cry anymore because I was so tired. I couldn't protect myself from my mom's beatings, but I tried as hard as I could, to protect my siblings from them.

It wasn't just me she told those horrible things to. When Jio was in elementary school, I was getting him ready to go to Mama Gwen's house. That's what he called my mom. He said he didn't want to go. I thought that was odd. Most grandkids love their grandparents and want to spend time with them. Grandparents tend to spoil their grandkids. They let them get away with things that they'd never allow their own children to get away with. They grow soft in their old age. So, I needed to figure out why he didn't want to go to my mom's. When I pushed Jio to tell me, he finally told me that he didn't like going over there because she said mean things to him and he felt sad. He said she told him she wished he was never born; that he was a bad boy. He cried. He begged me to please not make him go. It never occurred to me that my mom would be cruel to Jio like she'd been to me. I just presumed that she would treat her grandchildren better than she treated her children. That's what most grandparents do.

After listening to Jio, he didn't have to worry about my mom anymore. I wasn't going to subject my son to the same emotional torment that my mom reaped upon me. The question, for me, wasn't whether Jio would go to my mom's. The question was if I was going to allow my mom to have any kind of relationship with him. There was no way I was going to allow my mom to make my son feel unloved and unwanted. There was no way I ever wanted him to want to kill himself because of words she said, like I did. At least she was consistent. She'd said the same words to some of my siblings, as well.

Uchenna called me, when she was in 12th grade, I was maybe 23 years old, and told me she wanted to kill herself; that she couldn't take living with mama anymore. I told her she could come and live with me. She didn't want to, she only had one semester left and she wanted to graduate from Elsik with her friends. I begged her to just hold on. She only had one semester left; that she could leave and go to college and never come back and live with mama if she didn't want to. I told her suicide was a permanent solution to a temporary problem; that it would devastate everyone around her, including me.

Take it from me, I'm a child of suicide. I take threats of suicide seriously. I was willing to do anything I could, to help get my sister through her last semester of high school. She was both a great student and athlete. The world was her oyster. She shouldn't let mama take her future away. She made it through and graduated with honors and was all-state in sports, in the process. She went away to Baylor University and never looked back. She stayed away from Houston for almost a decade. While she was away, she earned an MBA. Ultimately she ended up attending medical school where she earned an MD, as well. She married and had four children.

Likewise, my other sister, thought about killing herself too, her senior year. I was 30. She called me desperate. She couldn't take life, with mama, anymore either. I gave her the same talking to that I gave Uchenna, but she took me up on my offer. She moved in with me her senior year. I bought her senior memorabilia, memories book, graduation invitations, and her prom stuff. I gave her lunch money. She graduated from Elsik and earned a full athletic scholarship to college and she never looked back either. She earned an accounting degree and is a small business owner. She also married and had two children.

I knew, oh so well, how my mom's words, wounded those she loved. I intended to protect Jio. I knew he'd be okay because I would make sure of it. I wanted him to have a relationship with his grandmother but with conditions. It would have to be healthy and positive and nurturing. There would be no negotiation about those terms. It was one of the hardest decisions I had to make as a parent: whether to keep my mom out of my son's life.

Needless to say, I didn't force Jio to go to my mom's. I stopped allowing him to visit. I just made up excuses for whenever she would ask when Jio was coming over. I didn't know how to speak with her about it, but I knew Jio wasn't lying to me. I just avoided that conversation with her. The same things Jio told me my mom said to him were the same things she said to me the whole time I was growing up. Jio wasn't going to have the same issues I had. No way. No how was I going to allow that to happen.

As luck would have it, I was asked to be on this local television show called The Debra Duncan Show. The topic of the show was "Overcoming Obstacles". By this time, I'd begun sharing with people that my dad committed suicide. Debra wrongly presumed that my dad's suicide was my biggest obstacle that I had to overcome. She asked me if I would come onto her show and talk with her about how I overcame my dad's suicide to be a successful lawyer. I thought long and hard about coming onto her show, but my appearance had to be about my authentic journey. My greatest obstacle wasn't my dad's suicide. The thing that most affected me, and in an unhealthy and negative way, was my relationship with my mom.

My mom's words were debilitating. They were lethal. They took away my joy. They caused me to attempt suicide. My only concern was airing "our dirty laundry" on television. But something inside of me, from the depths of my soul, told me that there might be other mothers and daughters out there, who had the same type of toxic relationship that my mom and I had. I knew that my mom's words negatively affected both of my sisters and my son. I knew it was a problem. I knew I needed to try and fix the problem, if at all possible.

I told Debra that the only way I would come onto her show was to discuss my biggest obstacle: my mom. She agreed that I could speak about it. I didn't want to surprise my mom by talking about our issues on local television without giving her a heads up. I didn't want her to think that I hated her because I didn't. I didn't want others to think that I hated her. I just wanted people to understand that moms could either help their children grow or devastate them to the point of suicide. Quite frankly, I didn't know if my mom even knew how debilitating she was to me. From outward appearances, it appeared that I was on top of the world but inside I was desperate for love. Trying to figure out if I was innately valuable; worthy of love, since my mom always told me that she wished that I was never born.

Even though I was an adult, it was like I was still a child. I needed guidance, so I called my grandmother and explained to her about the Debra Duncan invitation. I explained that my mom was my greatest obstacle and I needed to figure out how to broach the subject with her. Dear told me that she believed my mom loved me the best way she knew how; that there was no one right way parent; that all children are different, what works for one may not work for another. She believed that if I just spoke with my mom and told her how I felt that the healing could begin. I needed to speak with my mom first, before I committed to the appearance on the Debra Duncan Show. We needed to talk so I invited my mom over.

When my mom came to my home, it was awkward. We didn't have a close relationship. I'd learned to love my mom from a distance and not to expect her to unconditionally love and protect me. So, we weren't accustomed to having deep meaningful conversations. We didn't hug or kiss because she didn't hug or kiss me when I was young, so I'd learned to live without her affection. We didn't even sit down when she first walked in. We stood in the foyer and talked. I told her about the show. I explained to her that she was my greatest obstacle. I shared that it was time that we talked about our relationship because it was now affecting Jio; that's why he wasn't allowed to come to her house anymore; that I was tired of making up excuses about why Jio couldn't come over. I wasn't going to allow her to have my son trying to kill himself because of her cruel words. I just spilled a lot of my hurt and pain that I'd kept secret from her for over 30 years. I was forced to speak now because she was passing on her curse to my child, and as his parent, her behavior was unacceptable. I had to protect him from her, more specifically, from her words. We, she and I, needed to figure it out and move forward or move our separate ways. Dear called it ~ loving you from a distance.

I told her what Jio told me she said and that I believed him because what she told him is exactly what she'd said to me. That the words hurt me and that they hurt Jio. She apologized to me but said that she didn't remember actually saying the words. I was livid. What did she mean she didn't remember? How could she apologize for something she didn't remember? How could her apology be sincere? My mom's response was something to the effect that although she didn't have specific recollections of saying the cruel words to either me or Jio, that she knew she said it. I asked how she knew she said them if she didn't remember saying them? She said that it had to be true, because her mom said the exact same words to her. I asked her if the words hurt her when Mama Harriet said them to her? She said yes, the words hurt. I asked her why, if they hurt when Mama Harriet said them to her, then why did she say them to me? She answered that she didn't know any better.

That's how she was raised. That's what she learned from her mom, so she taught me the same way her mom taught her. I told my mom that if it hurts you then you shouldn't do the same things to your kids. She agreed. She told me she doesn't know why but that my success shone a light, to her, of her failures. It made her focus on all of her wrong decisions; consequently, she was jealous of my success even though she knew she shouldn't be. I thought that took tremendous courage for her to acknowledge that to me. She hadn't realized how much she'd hurt both Jio and me. Now that she had an understanding, she apologized and said she would try to do better. She agreed that we should talk about our issues on the Debra Duncan Show. My mom said if us talking about our relationship, on television, helped even one mother-daughter relationship be better, then it was worth it.

My mom, grandmother and Jio accompanied me on the Debra Duncan Show. My mom's attendance was a pleasant surprise. It was an awkward but necessary discussion. Debra still talked about my dad's suicide, but all in all, so many people thanked me for talking about my relationship with my mom. They said it helped them broach the subject with their moms. I was pleased. There were some who complained that I shouldn't have talked about my mom and that I was trying to put her down. That was never the point. Truthfully talking about real life obstacles is often times uncomfortable but necessary. That's one of the lessons I learned about owning my S.H.I.T! You can't ignore your S.H.I.T! less you're destined to repeat it. It repeated from my grandmother to my mother; from my mother to me, my sisters and my son. I was not going to do the same thing with my son. To do the same thing, over and over and expect a different result is insanity. I determined to own the unhealthiness of my relationship with my mom, address it to try and make it better, and if we couldn't make it better, then we would go our separate ways, and love each other from a distance. It was that simple. I owned that I was prepared to make a really tough decision, for both me and my son's mental health, and I was willing to stick to it.

The Debra Duncan Show began a process of my mom and I trying to redefine the type of relationship we would have. My mom started telling me that she loved me. Although those words were what I'd longed to hear for my entire life, hearing them then didn't satisfy the need I thought they would fill. She also started to try and hug and kiss me. Rather than evoking warm and fuzzy feelings of affection with my mom, her touch physically caused me to feel nauseated and extremely uncomfortable. I couldn't make myself hug her back. I think that over the years, my self-preservation instinct and need to not be emotionally hurt by her caused me to recoil from her physically. I learned how to not need her love or her touch. I was learning how to love myself. Dear is actually the person who helped me understand that I needed to love myself. I remember, when I was about 25 years old and I was crying, like I always did, about my mom not loving me. Dear asked me what I'd do if my mom never told me she loved me? She asked if I was going to cry for the rest of my life and be unhappy? She told me that I needed to prepare myself for that possibility. That if I couldn't get my mom's love and validation that I had to learn to love and validate my own self. I had to learn what I could and couldn't control. I could control myself, but I couldn't control my mom. That was the only way for me to be truly happy. She suggested that I accept that my mom and I might not have the idyllic relationship that I dreamed of and that I needed to figure out how to find happiness despite my disappointment. I took her up on her advice. I was tired of crying, almost every day. I had to begin to try and learn to love myself even if my mom didn't love me. I had to accept that I would have to define the parameters that I would deal with my mom. Once I accepted that my dream relationship with my mom was not to be, I had a new normal related to her. We had a relationship that wasn't intimate or trustworthy but that was okay. I didn't share secrets with her and that was okay too. I decided to meet her where she was. I stopped needing to her for my psychological and emotional well-being. It had to be that way. Once my frame of mind changed, the constant crying stopped. It was a new beginning or, so I hoped.

Chapter Nine

My Brother, Why, My Brother?

My Brother, Why, My Brother?
I ask this question of my race
Why do we insist on killing our own?
Don't we see we are the same standing face to face?

Why must a brother lay dead in the streets
For those remaining, a torrent of tears?
Senseless violence amongst our brothers
Will affect our people for years!

Why do our fathers make these brothers feel?
They have no bond with man to share?
Black men reach out to your sons
It is your responsibility to be there!

Why do our mothers teach our brothers to love through
love?
Have we not given them a swift hand?
While love is essential to their nurturing,
Discipline and respect, we must demand!

Why in our village of people?
Do we turn our backs and close our eyes?
Where our brother's future is lost
Undoubtedly our destiny lies!

Why does the future seem like nowhere to our brothers?
When will they learn they are one and the same?
Be strong willed and self-confident
Then your strength will uphold your name

Why am I brought to my knees?
Praying to someone above?
That our brothers will stop killing each other
And show one another some love

Why do we have to suffer and grieve?
Is it to understand a greater unity lost?
Regardless of the will, we must retrieve
No brother's life should be the cost

A deeper meaning to my brother's short life
Can't explain to my family the enormous hurt and pain
End this trend of violence young brothers
There are too many of you being slain!

My precious brother rest your soul
Be at peace
And brothers if you love at all
Please let this violence cease

For the sake of our future take heed
And protect and respect each other
Maybe then there will be no need to ask
My Brother, Why, My Brother?

I wrote this poem for my brother Chuck's funeral. I didn't want his death to be in vain. His life's choices both angered and disappointed me. It was very important for me to present this poem at his funeral. It's important for me to present it now. Why, you might ask? The different ways in which my brother and I dealt with the S.H.I.T! of our upbringing was literally the difference between life and death. This poem, written less than a week after he was murdered, was true then and is true now. Which if you think about it is sad. This ode to my brother, Chuck, deals with my family's S.H.I.T! specifically, but generally speaking, it addresses Black families across this nation and our relationship with Black on Black crime.

It was May 31, 1996. I was training for the 1996 United States Olympic Trials. The Olympics were to be in Atlanta that year. I had been retired from track and field for almost seven years. I'd won the 1989, US Heptathlon Championship. I was 23 years old. Now I was training for the 1990 track and field season with the specific purpose of defending my national title. I met Alejandro in early 1990. He pressured me to retire that same year. Therefore, I didn't defend my national title. I was 24 years old when I retired. It was now 1996. I had filed for divorce from Alejandro in November 1995, after he'd jumped on me for the last time. I was now 30, and a baby attorney at a prominent downtown law firm. I hadn't even been a lawyer for a year yet, but I took some time off to train. I wanted to make a comeback after being retired for almost seven years. The law firm I worked at helped raise money to help pay my bills since I wouldn't be earning a regular pay check at the firm. I was now officially a single parent. I had a lot on my plate, but I wanted to reclaim my life. Consequently, I started training, in March 1996. Everybody thought I was crazy. After laying off for so long, it was almost an impossible goal to qualify for the Olympic Trials. I trained hard and in my first meet, I surprisingly qualified for the Trials. I didn't have one of my best scores but only 16 people in the US qualified and I was proud to be in the top 16, considering my circumstances. Hopefully I was on the path to track and field greatness again.

I was on my way to practice, at UH, exactly two weeks, to the day, until the Heptathlon Trials were to begin, in Atlanta, when I received a call from my legal secretary. It was right around lunch time. She told me that someone in my family had died. I presumed it was my grandmother because she was in her late 70's and she was the oldest person in my family. My secretary told me that it wasn't my grandmother. I just knew it was Chuck. He was 19 years old and hustling for a living. I immediately called my mom. She was inconsolable. Her wailing was indescribable except to say that it came from the depths of her soul. Her favorite child was dead, murdered in the streets. She was hyperventilating. I knew I had to get to her, to my family. She needed to get off of the phone because of some emergency related to my baby brother. Even in the most traumatic of times, I'm super focused and responsible, so I needed to tell my coach that I had to miss practice that day. I drove rapidly yet calmly to the track and told my coach that I wouldn't be able to practice due to a family emergency. I didn't tell him my brother was murdered. I didn't feel like explaining anything. Apart from that, I didn't really know the details either. Nor had I processed it.

The timing of Chuck's murder couldn't have been worse, not that the timing of any murder, especially of a young person, is ever okay. I hadn't competed or trained at a high level in almost seven years. I really couldn't afford to miss any practices. My Olympic chances were a long shot already. Only the top three finishers at the Olympic Trials make the Olympic team and usually people train for years to be in Olympic-caliber condition, I'd had a scant three months of training. Truthfully, it was a miracle to qualify in two months for such a grueling event. For the record, the heptathlon is the female version of the decathlon. While the decathlon is ten track and field events, the heptathlon is seven, namely hurdles, high jump, shot put, and 200 meters on Day 1; and long jump, javelin, and 800 meters on Day 2. It was brutal and required exceptional conditioning and training, which I needed more of.

After I told my coach I couldn't practice, I headed for my mom's house. Driving as fast as I could but also as safe as I could. I was screaming and pounding my fists against the steering wheel and dash board. I remember yelling at Chuck, as if he could hear me. Why Chuck, why? You know better! Why'd you have to go and get yourself killed? Oh my God, Momma's going to die! She can't live without you! You're her favorite! I warned you! I told you the last time I spoke with you that your lifestyle was going to get you locked up! S.H.I.T!, I didn't think it would get you killed! My conversation with Chuck was at times, angry, at times sorrow-filled, at times, guttural. I was wailing and felt so helpless as it related to saving him, but I was trying to figure out how to save my family. I knew that my family would be falling apart. It's always been my role, in my family, and on my sports team, to be the calm during the storm. I knew my mom was grief-stricken. I'd already spoken with her. My baby sister had just graduated from high school, she and Chuck were a year and three days a part. They were super close. I knew she would be devastated. My baby brother looked up to Chuck, in a family full of women, those two were each other's ride or die. He was 14 years old.

Uchenna was home for India's graduation. I didn't really think about Greg because I held him responsible for a lot of the issues Chuck had. I had to get to my mom's as fast as I could. I wondered what happened? How did it happen? When did it happen? I cried, yelled and screamed the whole way to my mom's. I had to get it out now before I got there. I couldn't be falling apart in front of them. Because we couldn't all be falling apart together. I was the glue. I was the oldest. About five minutes from my mom's house, I stopped crying, dried my tears, blew my nose, and put on my game face. It was time to be focused; the fixer. When I drove up, my sisters and my mom were there. Predictably, they were devastated. Everyone was crying and screaming and trying to make sense of what we'd just learned. Chuck was dead. I didn't see Ulmer, where was Ulmer? I thought it odd that he wasn't there. Ulmer had left and said he was going to find Damian, Chuck's friend who was reportedly with Chuck when he got shot. Ulmer intended to kill Damian. He blamed him for Chuck dying. In Ulmer's mind, Damian should never have left Chuck. If Damian hadn't left Chuck, then Chuck wouldn't be dead. Someone had gone to get Ulmer and bring him back. It may have been Greg. I was worried about Ulmer. What could a 14-year-old boy do to a 19-year-old man? In my mind, nothing. At some point, someone brought Ulmer back. He was crying and so angry and screaming that he was going to kill Damian. I was trying to talk sense into him. He couldn't kill Damian.

He had to calm down. If he killed Damian, then he'd go to jail. If he went to jail then he would miss Chuck's funeral. Ulmer had to be watched carefully because he kept trying to leave to go find Damian. We couldn't let that happen. It was a chaotic time. We were definitely trapped in a nightmare, except for, it wasn't a dream. I remember us being outside, them yelling and screaming and me trying to talk everyone off whatever their cliff they were on.

India was crying, just screaming why, Chuck, why? What happened? Calling his name and saying my brother is gone. She was both inconsolable and in disbelief. Obviously, Uchenna was the same. She just so happened to be in town, from Waco, she was working on her MBA at Baylor University, for India's high school graduation. For the most part, my siblings hadn't really experienced death, especially of a young person, much less a sibling. Some of our grandparents had died but they were old. Old people die. That's to be expected. I, on the other hand, had experienced a lot of death, and was old enough to have had experience with grieving.

I learned that that my mom had gotten a call from Damian. He'd told my mom that he believed that Chuck got shot. He wasn't sure if Chuck was okay. Damian had to flee the scene. He told my mom where Chuck was, in some apartments in Southwest Houston that just so happened to be near apartments our cousins lived in. My mom called my cousin and begged him to go over to the apartments to see if Chuck was okay. Both cousins went over and one of them identified the body. It was Chuck. I later found out from my cousin, the position of his body and that he was laying in what looked like a "lake or pool" of blood. To this day, she's traumatized. She was 17 years old. She'd actually lived at my mom's house for a while, so she'd grown up with Chuck.

Each verse of the poem had meaning to me. Immediately after my brother died, I was grieving and trying to understand what happened? What led to this? I had ideas about who may have contributed to Chuck's death. *My Brother, Why,*

My Brother? was my attempt to conceptualize the road map to his death.

Verse 1:

> *"My Brother, Why, My Brother?*
> *I ask this question of my race*
> *Why do we insist on killing our own?*
> *Don't we see we are the same standing face to face?"*

I had questions. I didn't understand. Why did Black people kill Black people? Chuck wasn't the first Black man to be killed by someone who looked just like him. Who was Black like him. Who was in the same situation like him. Who was poor like him. Who had things in common with him. Who was trying to make it out of poverty like him. Although I didn't know who specifically killed Chuck, at that time, I knew deep down in my heart that it was Black on Black crime. It was something I was familiar with from an early age.

I was introduced to my first bullet when I was less than five years old. I was playing outside in the yard at Dear's house. I heard pops. I didn't know what it was, so I ran towards the sound. I saw a man run by the front of Dear's house, on Scott Street, as fast as he could. He was running away from something. I was about to step around the corner to see what was going on. The next thing I knew, Aunt Camille grabbed me and ran dragging me into the house. Away from the shots. She was yelling at me telling me, the whole time, that I could've gotten shot and killed. That you never run towards gun shots. Aunt Camille was about 12 years old. We hear so many stories of innocent bystanders, even children, getting shot while doing normal everyday things, like playing outside or sleeping in your home. I could've been an innocent bystander. A statistic. Collateral damage.

I saw my first dead body, laying on the sidewalk, two houses from my grandmother's house. I was probably seven or eight years old. Dear had just picked up my cousins, my aunts and me, from Astroworld, a Six Flags amusement park that used to be in Houston. As a side note, Travis Scott, the famous rapper, singer, song writer and producer, named his album and music festival after Astroworld. In any case, we were just getting home. As we drove up to park in the driveway, people in the neighborhood were gathered around something. There was a commotion. I was always a curious child so I jumped out of the station wagon a ran to see what everybody was looking at. When I squeezed through the crowd, I saw a man lying on his back on the sidewalk. He looked like he was asleep. I was standing right next to him. His eyes were closed. The next thing I knew, my grandmother had grabbed me by arm and dragged me away, chastising me, "doggonit, Sweetheart, come with me, you shouldn't have come over here." I asked why that man was lying on the street. She told me that it was "none of my business." I remember coming outside to play the next day and seeing the blood that was left. I hadn't seen the blood the night before. Now I know, since I'm a criminal defense lawyer, that he must've been shot in the front and the puddle of blood that remained was from the exit wound.

People in my family had been victims of Black on Black crime. In high school, my Aunt Daphne had been murdered. She was my dad's sister. She'd been shot two times in the head and thrown off of the second story of a crack house which is interestingly less than five minutes from where I live now.

In college, my cousin Warren was murdered. He hadn't been hustling or gang-banging. He was from Los Angeles. He was a business professional. Successful. The crème de la crème of our family. He'd graduated from an Ivy League University and went on to earn a graduate degree, pledged a fraternity, and was a Black belt in karate. He was a part of the Black elite community in Atlanta. He'd been robbed and died.

There's no need for me to go on and on about the Black on Black crime I knew and that touched me and my family. I just knew that I didn't understand why we were killing each and that it needed to stop. We needed to talk about it. To get to the bottom of it, if at all possible. I wanted to start my family and friend's discussion at Chuck's funeral.

Verse 2:

"Why must a brother lay dead in the streets
For those remaining, a torrent of tears?
Senseless violence amongst our brothers
Will affect our people for years!"

I knew Chuck's death would have long lasting, perhaps, ever lasting effects on my family. I knew that death was permanent. I knew that from my dad. That you can't go back. You don't get a do over. He was only 19. He had so much left undone, yet he died a senseless death. He'd put himself in a perilous situation that he created on his own, for no good reason, at least not in my mind. He chose the quick way out of poverty, not the more carefully planned and stable way out, namely education or sports. All of us, my mom's kids, all lived in the same house, with the same mom, under similar conditions ~ at times, no lights, no water, no food, no new clothes, no whatever. We all lived through evictions and embarrassment. My sisters and I chose education, Chuck chose the hustle. His hustling put him in harm's way. I thought he'd end up in prison, not dead. He ended up like so many other young Black men, for no reason other than they were impatient. He/they wanted what they wanted now. He/They took what they wanted. He/They skipped school. He/They broke into people's homes and cars. He/They robbed each other. He/They stole from family. He/They lied. He/They smoked weed, dipped Swisher Sweets in formaldehyde, and sold crack.

In my sad yet respectful opinion, Chuck's most lasting legacy was that he intentionally, or accidentally, inspired our baby brother, to choose the path of anger and despair. Ulmer's hope was lost the moment the news of Chuck's death was disclosed to him. Consequently, Ulmer has sold drugs and used drugs to self-medicate the pain away. He started with weed, graduated to crack and then to PCP. The weed and PCP were just like Chuck. It's also put Ulmer in a mind space where he felt sorry for himself and his life. He's had a victim mentality and I attribute that to Chuck. So whether Chuck knew it or not, he modeled bad behavior for his younger brother. To this day, my sister's and I can't speak about Ulmer without talking about Chuck's death and its destructive effect on him. I remember a conversation with India and I had about Ulmer. To this day, we constantly have family drama related to him and my mom. India commented that she felt sorry for Ulmer because he's been unable to recover from Chuck's death. He's been angry since the day Chuck was murdered. I responded to her that Chuck was all of our brother, and we turned out okay. India lamented that Ulmer and Chuck were especially close because they were the two boys to our three girls and since Ulmer, is the baby, that he looked up to Chuck, unlike the rest of us. She believed they the boys had a special bond that the girls couldn't understand.

I guess I can see her point but what do you do when someone can't seem to turn the corner over something that happened over 20 years ago? Chuck's death has definitely defined Ulmer's life. I guess Ulmer also was at a tender age, 14, and his childhood was shattered. Before Chuck's death, Ulmer was happy, go-lucky and funny as hell with not a care in the world. After Chuck's death, Ulmer is angry, an addict with a criminal record, who lives with our mom and always finds it difficult to find and keep a job. To me, Chuck's death is sad and senseless, and eternal. I hope one day that Ulmer identifies his S.H.I.T!, owns it and positively gets through it but that remains to be seen.

For Jiovanni, who was four years old, I wanted him to remember Chuck and the finality and brutality of his death for years. Actually forever. So, I made a decision to take Jio to the funeral home before Chuck was cleaned up for the funeral. I showed him Chuck's dead body and all five bullet wounds, including the two in his head. Some thought I shouldn't have done that, but I knew I needed Jio to have a clear understanding that there's nothing glorious or heroic about death. That it cold and ugly and final. And that the uncle that he loved and adored and who loved and adored him was never coming back and it was all because of bad decisions that his uncle made. I hoped that it would always stick in the back of his mind that if he made the wrong decisions that he could end up dead. I'd tried to do the same thing to Chuck about six months before he was murdered. Now let me be clear, it didn't occur to me that Chuck would be killed. I thought his actions would land him in prison. I didn't know he was jacking drug dealers at the time. I thought he was just stealing people's stuff.

The straw that'd broken the camel's back, for me, was that Chuck had stolen most of my Nike gear and some of my USA Track and Field team warmups, and other warmups that I had traded from other national teams, like Korea and Great Britain and Japan. It's common for athletes around the world to trade uniforms. I'd competed in many international competitions, representing the US like the World University Games, the Pan Am Games, and had exchanged sweats with various athletes from other countries. When I moved to Spain, I left my belongings with my mom. She was supposed to keep them for me until I was stable and had my own place. I'd been distracted from my path by the abusive relationship I had with Alejandro, so my mom had my belongings at her house.

I had been a Nike athlete since the Olympic Trials in 1984, when I was in high school. I got free Nike gear the entire time I was in college and it was always the latest gear and I got it prior to the public getting it. I prized those national team warmups and Nike gear. I'd earned them. They were my memorabilia. My keepsakes. I was going to leave them for Jio. When I finally fled my abusive marriage, I found a place to stay and when I went to go get my things, I learned that Chuck had sold my stuff. I was so angry and disappointed. Chuck had called me for something and showed up at my house. I told him he was no longer welcomed at my home. That I didn't approve of his lifestyle and disrespect of me and my possessions. They weren't his to sell. That stealing my stuff was unacceptable. That having to explain to Jio where his uncle was every time Chuck got locked up was unacceptable. It was important for me to change the trajectory of the lives of Jones men. Most of my uncles got locked up, and with the exception of my dad who attended college but blew his brains out before he graduated, no Jones man had gone to college. The only successful Jones man was my grandfather, and that was limited to business. It was my plan to change that curse for Jio. I often told Jio that he was going to be successful, even if it killed him. In other words, I was going to do whatever I had to do to teach Jio right from wrong, even if it hurt Jio by me having to spank him. That was my job. And as I explained to Chuck, there was no way I was going to allow Jio to be in his life as he was living it. Jio looked up to Chuck. He loved his uncle Chuck. I couldn't. No, I wouldn't allow Chuck to set a bad example for Jio. No way. No how. I told Chuck that I loved him but that we, Jio and I, would love him from a distance until he got his life together and started making better decisions. I told him that I loved him, but it was time for tough love. I explained that whenever he was ready to change his way of life that I would be the first one to help but he had to make a change. I hugged and kissed him and that was that. I was 30 years old. He was 19. That was the last time I spoke with my brother.

Verse 3:

> *"Why do our fathers make these brothers feel*
> *They have no bond with man to share?*
> *Black men reach out to your sons*
> *It is your responsibility to be there!"*

This verse was specifically dedicated to Greg, Chuck and Ulmer's dad, and other men like him. Greg wasn't really around when Chuck and Ulmer were young. When he was around, he was a player and treated my mom horribly and disrespectfully. He was a womanizer and so was Chuck. He chased women. So, did Chuck. It's my understanding, from a number of Chuck's friends, that I spoke with after his death, that women were one of the drivers of Chuck's hustle, which was jacking drug dealers. He needed the money to dress well and get girls. He and his crew used to wear boots like Jodeci, so they called themselves the "Boot Crew", with their pants tucked into their boots. There were contests to see who could have sex with the most women. When your focus is that the more women you have is directly indicative of how good of a man you are, then you've been taught the wrong lesson.

I know Chuck resented Greg because we talked about it. He didn't respect that Greg wasn't around consistently as a father. Greg bounced back into their lives when Chuck was a teenager and tried to play daddy. Chuck didn't respect his dad. He also had to hustle because Greg didn't provide financially for my mom or his kids, Chuck and Ulmer. Arguably Greg didn't provide emotionally either. Greg, specifically, and other fathers generally, need to really evaluate who and what they're teaching their sons to be. It was Greg's responsibility to be there for Chuck and Ulmer. He failed and now he's got one dead son and one broken son. That makes me sad and angry. There's nothing I can do about it, with respect to Ulmer, until he decides to own his S.H.I.T! When and if he does that, I'll be the first one to try and assist him.

Verse 4:

"Why do our mothers teach our brothers to love through love?
Have we not given them a swift hand?
While love is essential to their nurturing,
Discipline and respect, we must demand!"

I've always said my mom raised her daughters to be self-sufficient, but she loved her sons and enabled their irresponsibility and refusal to accept or recognize that there are consequences for bad behavior. That holds true for a lot of people. Prime example: I got beat for making 97-A's instead of

100-A's. I got punished, for the whole summer, I couldn't go outside and play, for getting my first "B" in the fifth grade. I couldn't miss school, even if I was sick, because she drilled in me that grades were my only way out of poverty; consequently, I had perfect attendance through grade school, except for eight grade, when I was told, the day before awards day that I wasn't getting a perfect attendance award because I'd missed a day of school. I pleaded my point that I hadn't missed a day. They didn't believe me. I called myself showing them, that if I wasn't getting perfect attendance, because I'd missed a day of school, then I was going to actually miss a day of school. So I skipped school on awards day. As it turns out, they realized their mistake and did call out my name for a "Perfect Attendance" award and I wasn't there. I got beat by my mom for not going to school. Yet with Chuck, she wanted him to go to school but didn't require him to be responsible for his attendance at school. India, who was a year younger than him was required to get Chuck to school or else she'd get in trouble. Rather than comment, I'll let you think about the hypocrisy of that. If I talked back to my mom, I'd get hit in the mouth, I heard Chuck talk back all the time with no consequences. I even hear Ulmer talk back now. When I shoplifted as a kid, my mom told people I was a thief yet when Chuck started getting in trouble in his teens all she did was make excuses for his bad behavior, "it wasn't his fault. He was at the wrong place at the wrong time with the wrong people." It was never Chuck's fault. I was always "everybody else's fault". And, she'd literally begged for money to pay Chuck's bond or for a lawyer, for him, before she'd pay her rent or utilities. I remember once my mom not having water for seven months at the house. Another time my mom found numerous weapons and identification cards in her attic. When I asked my mom what she meant by weapons, she described them as "big, long machine guns." She hadn't counted them there were so many. I was surprised that she didn't put Chuck out of the house considering how much she was terrified of guns. Her fear of guns dated back to my dad's suicide. She'd even taught me to be afraid of guns. The police hadn't found the guns. She'd actually found them after the police had torn up the house, found nothing and left. Then she had the nerve to ask me to borrow money to hire a lawyer for Chuck because she knew he was going to need one. She always covered for him and tried to find explanations for his behavior. She didn't blast him publicly for his obviously serious criminal behavior, yet she publicly humiliated me over me shoplifting a pair of jeans when I was 16. She had a double standard. Chuck could never do wrong and if he did, then he was forgiven. That wasn't the case for me.

My mom raised my sisters and me to know that we, and only ourselves individually, would take care of us. My mom didn't raise my brothers the same way. She loved my brothers to the point that she didn't teach them to be responsible for themselves. She loved them and taught them that a woman will always bail you out, pun intended, and never hold you accountable. Chuck, up until the time he died, and Ulmer up until now, both never worried about consequences for their actions because they knew my mom would always get them out of any trouble they got in to, and if she didn't have whatever it took to bail them out, then she would beg and borrow and not pay bills, to figure it out. That's not the way to raise a son or a grandson.

When Jio was little, when he would get in trouble with me and I'd punish him, he would go whine to my mom. At first, I didn't know how to tell my mom to back off and stop chastising my parenting in front of Jio. I literally got up the nerve, to finally tell her to stand down. I advised her that, respectfully, she didn't do a good job with her sons, one was dead and the other has a criminal record and can't keep a job and is an addict, and those weren't the kind of lives, I was raising Jio to achieve. Therefore, she wasn't allowed to interfere with my ability to raise my son nor interfere with my ability to teach him that there are consequences for actions. If she insisted on trying to undermine my authority, as his mom, then she wouldn't be allowed to be in his life. Period. Point blank. If she had any concerns about my parenting then she could pull me aside, outside of Jio's eye-shot and ear-shot and share her perspective. I would take what she said under advisement, if I so chose. And regardless of whether I took her advice or not, she should respect my decision. If we didn't have that agreement, then she wouldn't be allowed to be in Jio's life. I felt then and still feel now that that was a life or death decision, I made for Jio as it related to my mom. I let her know in no uncertain terms that "I'm his momma, you aren't!" I didn't stutter. I didn't mumble. I was matter-of-fact. I meant it. I knew she was consciously or subconsciously creating S.H.I.T! for me and Jio and I owned it and addressed it before it became a big problem.

Verse 5:

> *"Why in our village of people*
> *Do we turn our backs and close our eyes?*
> *Where our brother's future is lost*
> *Undoubtedly our destiny lies!"*

During segregation, I understood that the Black community knew that the only way to save our community was for us to live the old African proverb that it takes a village to raise a child. By way of example, one time that I was at one of my nephew's birthday party and one of my cousins, who was less than ten years old, was beating up another of our little cousins. As a responsible adult, I grabbed his hands to stop him from hitting his cousin. I tried to explain that we were family and shouldn't fight each other. That we win as a family. That we lose as a family. And that family should have each other's back. Rather than be supportive, some of my other family members told me to let him go. That his mom would be angry at me for touching her child. I held his hands tightly because he was literally trying to fight me to get to his cousin to beat him up. I refused to let go. I implored my family that we had to teach him to keep his hands to himself. The next thing you know he was threatening to kill me. I couldn't believe what I was hearing. One of my cousins warned me that his mom was on her way and she said she "was going to beat my ass". I let him go because, notwithstanding my professional credentials, I wasn't going to "catch a case" over some dumb family S.H.I.T!, but I warned that if he continued to be violent and no one taught him right from wrong, at such an impressionable age, that one day he would either 1) kill somebody, 2) be killed by somebody he tried to fight, or 3) go to prison. Needless to say, some of my predictions have manifested. In that instance, the village didn't stand with me. I wonder, to this day, had we as a family stood together, if my cousin's life would be different.

Our family's S.H.I.T! has continued to manifest, despite small successes by some of us, but I firmly believe it takes a village. After integration, we, as Black people, lost that strong foundational philosophy that we must work together as a people. We somehow evolved into a crab in the bucket mentality whereby we drag each other down rather than trying to lift each other up. The refrain stopped being "we" and instead became "me". We lost the ability to see the humanity in "us". When we did that it became easier to hurt others without blinking an eye. Our inability to see the humanity in our race is the S.H.I.T! that is literally killing us. I firmly believe that if we'd only accept our S.H.I.T!, figure out how to deal with our S.H.I.T! positively, while helping each other, then respect would grow, and our race would necessarily be uplifted. And then, we wouldn't be killing each other.

Verse 6:

"Why does the future seem like nowhere to our brothers?
When will they learn they are one and the same?
Be strong willed and self-confident
Then your strength will uphold your name"

I have instilled in Jio, to teach one by reaching one, especially as it relates to our family. Jio has taken this to heart.

He mentors at-risk elementary schools' boys who don't have positive male role models in their lives, and he mentors his younger cousins to do positive things. One of the things he teaches them is the importance of goal setting, both short- and long-term goals. In my family, we don't have enough of that, but I also think that we, as Black people, don't do enough mentoring each other, regardless of biological relations. I know Chuck's "mentoring" of Ulmer created a misguided boy who grew into a dysfunctional man, although the term "man" is questionable. Chuck lived for the day, not the long term. I thought that was a fatal flaw, pun also intended. Because he didn't plan for the future, he died in the present and his memory is stuck in the past.

Verse 7:

"Why am I brought to my knees
Praying to someone above?
That our brothers will stop killing each other
And show one another some love"

I suspect my mom was praying for Chuck before he was murdered but I know, for certain, that I heard her crying out for God's help in understanding why Chuck died. I even heard people saying they were mad at God for allowing Chuck to die. Well, I firmly believe that God gives us free will for a reason, to see if we will do good or bad. He will not save us from our bad decisions just like he didn't stop Adam and Eve from eating the apple in the Garden of Eden. God helps those who help themselves. So, my question to my mom and others like her, is, why everything is asked of God when nothing is asked of the person they're praying for. That seems oxymoronic to me. When I asked my mom to discipline Chuck, as she disciplined us; to be as strict with Chuck as she was with us, she refused. I believe so many people, including my mom, blame God for things that are the responsibility of the Chuck's of the world. It seems to me that the prayers and anger at God are really meant as comfort for those left living rather than for the deceased persons. When my brother was alive, I kept thinking that all of the praying in the world wasn't going to save him from his repeated bad decisions. When he was murdered, I thought that all of the praying in the world wasn't going to bring him back. The S.H.I.T! that could've saved Chuck wasn't owned before his death. That's the thing about owning your S.H.I.T!, it only works for the living. I wanted the people attending the funeral to be warned that praying to God alone, without requiring the person you're praying for to be accountable, won't protect that person from peril nor will it raise the dead. That the urgency is now. Eventually your S.H.I.T! will kill you if you don't own it. You've got to fix yourself.

Verse 8:

> *"Why do we have to suffer and grieve?*
> *Is it to understand a greater unity lost?*
> *Regardless of the will, we must retrieve*
> *No brother's life should be the cost"*

This verse is rhetorical. It's challenging the reader to figure out his/her own solution to us killing each other. No matter how many ways you look at it, there is no greater understanding to be gained with each death. Our boys and men will continue to die and we will continue to suffer and grieve so long as we keep ignoring our S.H.I.T! and refusing to hold them and ourselves accountable. It's that simple.

Verse 9:

> *"A deeper meaning to my brother's short life*
> *Can't explain to my family the enormous hurt and pain*
> *End this trend of violence young brothers*
> *There are too many of you being slain!"*

There is no deeper meaning and even if there is, it's not going to stop the hurt. The pain and loss will be enormous regardless so we, Black people, need to own our own S.H.I.T! or this cycle is doomed to repeat itself. There's no guarantee to a long life. In the simplest of terms: If you continually do dumb S.H.I.T! then bad S.H.I.T! happens to you. The more our young men continue to engage in this type of behavior and the more we allow it, then the numbers will continue to grow. Truth is, one death of a young man is too much, so at some point you see so much death, that it becomes the new normal. Sort of like after the jury saw Rodney King get beat, over and over, it was desensitized; therefore, what the police did to Mr. King was normalized. I saw that writing on the wall with my brother. Rather than being deterred from bad behavior each time he got in trouble, my mom would try and minimize the negative consequences by either bailing him out or hiring him a lawyer. Consequently, he became more comfortable with his reckless behavior. She was his greatest enabler. Plain and simple. It sounds harsh but it's the truth. The only meaning you need to figure out, in this verse, is to own your part of the negative outcome. See what you could've done better. Then, don't make the same mistake, to be an enabler, a non-discipliner, with the next young Black man. Push the next young Black man you encounter, who is behaving badly, to recognize his S.H.I.T! To own his S.H.I.T! To both be better and do better. Don't enable him. Don't take no for an answer. Own your responsibility as a part of the village.

Verse 10:

> *"My precious brother rest your soul*
> *Be at peace*
> *And brothers if you love at all*
> *Please let this violence cease"*

I was hoped and prayed that Chuck was going to Heaven, but I wasn't certain. But I still wanted my brother to have as much peace, in death, as possible. I knew my mom was probably thinking about where Chuck was in the afterlife. But I really wanted to young men, my brother's friends who attended his funeral, to have permission or awareness that if they are capable of love then they are capable of ending the violence and death. They needed to learn how to own the love and thrive off of it. Rather than looking at love as a weakness. I wondered if they ever worried about dying young. There's no way a person can have peace while simultaneously looking over your shoulder. I hoped to help them understand that they had the power to stop these funerals. I know Damian, the friend who was with Chuck when he died, practically hugged Chuck out of his casket. He had to be made to let Chuck go and to leave the casket. I could tell that he somehow felt responsible for Chuck being there. I could tell that he wished things had worked out differently. That he could've effected a different outcome had he made better decisions. He was wailing and apologizing to Chuck. I wanted all of Chuck's homeboys to know they could stop it, if they owned their S.H.I.T!

Verse 11:

>*"For the sake of our future take heed*
>*And protect and respect each other*
>*Maybe then there will be no need to ask*
>*My Brother, Why, My Brother?"*

I hoped that if the attendees at the funeral actually listened to the words of the poem, and truly reflected upon them, notwithstanding the harshness of the words, that their active listening and reflection would be the first step to owning their S.H.I.T! That reflection on Chuck's death, was most poignant, at his funeral, with his body, in that casket, before their very eyes, at that moment in time. I didn't want his death to be in vain. I wanted to drop seeds of introspection and raise the contradictions of the manner in which they lived their lives.

If they really thought about it then they'd see that they might very well be next person laying in the coffin.

I committed the poem to memory so that I could deliver it powerfully. Nowadays we call it spoken word. I thought the message needed to be heard and at no better time than the present. I thought some feelings might be hurt but I didn't care. In my estimation, people's feelings should've been hurt that Chuck was dead and that there were others, probably waiting in line to be next, quickly, if they continued to engage in the same reckless behavior. I wanted people to not just focus on mourning. I've had so many family members die young due to reckless behavior that predictably leads to prison or death or both. The deaths in my family continue.

I had a cousin murdered when I was on city council, which ironically, I'd given a lecture on Black on Black that very day. I was notified via a text, after the lecture, that read: "Randall got killed". My family had gathered at the apartment complex where he was murdered waiting for the medical examiner to come and retrieve his body. As macabre as it was, some people were actually taking cell phone pictures of his corpse. I asked a guy who was taking pictures of my cousin to please not take pictures of my dead cousin. I begged him to please give him some dignity in death. Police officers were everywhere. Some were laughing and joking, which I certainly didn't see any humor in my cousin's dead body lying in the parking lot. Some looked irritated for having to be there. I asked an assistant chief to see if he could re-situate the police cars as to block the view of my cousin's body so people couldn't take photos any more. I also asked the assistant chief to get his officers there to at least pretend to be professional and stop laughing and joking. I'd noticed some people staring at me until someone eventually asked me, "hey, ain't you that lady on TV?" I answered, "yes, that's me, and the dead guy you're taking cell phone pictures of is my cousin. Do you think, maybe, that you could stop taking pictures and give my cousin some dignity in death?" That was weird. I couldn't help but see the oxymoronic nature of me, a sitting city council member, standing at the crime scene of my murdered cousin, after having given a lecture on Black on Black crime. My dead cousin's dad was one of my dad's brothers who committed suicide. My uncle's suicide profoundly and negatively affected my cousin's life.

I've had other members of my family murdered too but I won't talk about them, except to say that it's the same story, different verse. That's why it was important to talk about Chuck's death. I hope and pray that we, as a people, can use my brother's death as a clarion call to evaluate what we, as Black people, can do to stop the tsunami of Black on Black crime. We, as Black people, have to own our S.H.I.T! This is our community, collectively and individually. My mom raised me on African culture, which was a part of the S.H.A.P.E Community Center philosophy. As a part of that training, I learned this which is called "The Circle of Interdependence":

"I am because we are
We are therefore I am
There's no me without you
And there's no you without me
We are all a part of a family of interdependence"

I swear by it. Believe me when I say that if we, as Black people, don't understand this basic truth to be self-evident, that we are indelibly linked whether we accept it or not, then we are doomed to continue down the same path. We must own and accept the importance of us all working together collectively. If we do not, then we are the very definition of insanity. We can't keep doing things the same way and to expect a different result. This gang banging has got to stop. It leads to the grave. We've got to own our collective S.H.I.T! or we're destined to continue to lose too many young Black men to Black on Black crime. This is a part of me owning my S.H.I.T! Have you owned yours?

Chapter Ten

Mistaking Jealousy For Love

If someone would've bet me money that I would be in an abusive relationship before I actually was in one, I would've lost that bet. I would've never guessed that I would've stayed with an abuser after he first laid his hands on me; that I would've made a baby with him, much less married him but I'm guilty of all of the above. Mind you, this is hind sight, and it's 20/20. As I travel the United States, sharing my domestic abuse and violence experience, a consistent theme of audiences is their inability to understand why I, Jolanda Jones, a really strong and accomplished woman, stayed with an abusive man or that I "let someone whoop my you-know-what" with all of my intelligence, resources and physical strength. I'm not the first and won't be the last person to be abused by the person they love unfortunately. But this chapter is an effort to explain this cycle of domestic abuse phenomenon. It's a story I've started to share because this ugly little secret needs to be outed in order to learn to identify it, deal with it and ultimately, how to stop it. This is a potentially life or death discussion.

While there are high profile domestic violence deaths like Lacy Peterson, Nicole Brown Simpson, Ron Goldman, a pregnant Shanann Watts and her two daughters, there are lesser known domestic violence deaths like Lashonda Childs and Tynesha Stewart. Nearly three women per day, in the US, are killed by intimate partners. Regardless of where the domestic violence occurs, we all have similar stories. The big difference being that I was able to get out alive. As I said before, hindsight is 20/20 because it's so clear now that the almost six years I was with Alejandro, were the most non-productive years of my life. For the most part, during that period, my most important job was just trying to survive. I merely existed. I didn't live. It was a period that some people will judge me negatively on, but it was also probably a period in my life that taught me how to eventually love myself through learning to own my S.H.I.T! Like me, some women have been lucky enough to get out alive. The best way to figure out how to help someone escape safely, is for you to understand why we stay in abusive relationships and don't tell.

For me, sharing this experience first began during the case against OJ Simpson, then charged with killing Nicole Brown Simpson and Ron Goldman. For the record, when I first shared "my" story I referred to the situation as having happened to someone other than me. I didn't own my story. My S.H.I.T! I just gave my third party "observation" about Nicole's situation. At the time, I was a baby lawyer, in the civil litigation section, of a very prominent law firm in Houston. I was the first Black law clerk and lawyer at the firm. Our firm was as mesmerized by the "Trial of the Century" as everyone else in the country, and our firm didn't practice criminal law. [Note: I have now been practicing criminal law for over 20 years]. We all had opinions on what happened and what the result of the trial would be. Everyone freely gave their opinions. Unbeknownst to everyone in the firm, I was then currently involved with an abusive man - my now ex-husband, Alejandro. We had been together for approximately four years. We had a child together.

In any case, three male attorneys, one a partner and the other two, associates like me, and I were in the elevator bank waiting for an elevator. We had been discussing the OJ case as we waited. The partner commented that while it might have been OJ's fault when the first beating happened, Nicole's death was her fault. It was her fault because after the first beating, she should've left him. He said she was stupid; that her lack of education probably played a part. The other associate attorneys all nodded in agreement. I didn't. I was silent. I had my poker face on. He continued with something like, "Right Jo, don't you agree? I mean you're a strong woman. You wouldn't have stood for that, right?!" I remember feeling really trapped.

It's amazing how many thoughts can go through your mind in a split second. I thought, "But I don't agree. It's not Nicole's fault. If I tell them, they won't respect me. These are my colleagues. You don't talk about personal stuff at work. They'll think I'm weak. They'll think I'm stupid. Will the firm fire me?"

Although I was afraid, before I knew it my words came out and so did the truth. I said with conviction, "No, actually I don't agree with you, respectfully." They all had looks of surprise on their faces. I appeared to be the epitome of strength and accomplishment. The partner immediately asked me why? The words continued to flow, and it went something like this:

Do any of you have a mother? A sister? A grandmother? A niece? A daughter? They all answered "yes" to some or all of my questions. I continued. Have any of you done things you were ashamed of, and hope the world never learns about? It's the secret that you will take with you to the grave? The secret that people will negatively judge you for but it's not what defines you? That maybe you're ashamed of something you did? They nodded "yes" again, to at least some of my questions. I asked them if they loved these women in their lives. "Yes" again they nodded. I continued. What if the only mistake either of them made in life was to fall in love with an abusive man? I asked the partner, because I knew he had a daughter. Would you agree that children want to please their parents, even when they're fifty years old? Children don't want to disappoint their parents. Children don't want for parents to think they're stupid. Children, no matter what age, are sometimes insecure.

The bottom line is, if you're the parent or friend or relative who's spouting off about how it's all Nicole's fault, I promise you, your daughter or sister or mother or friend WILL NOT tell you. You know why? Because when you make Blame-The-Victim-Comments like it's the victim's fault or she's stupid or she deserved what she got because she didn't leave, you're inviting your daughter, sister, mother or friend to stay in that relationship. She's not going to ask for your help;

not necessarily because she doesn't want to, but because she doesn't want to be talked down to; or she's already embarrassed; or she's already ashamed; or she doesn't want to disappoint you; or she doesn't want to be judged. And that decision, based on her fears of disappointing you, may lead her to be the next Nicole Brown Simpson.

You should blame the person who deserves the blame, the abuser. It's never right to abuse someone, no matter how angry you become. No matter how much you think she made you mad. Who knows, maybe she was leaving him and that's why he killed her. Statistics show that women are in the most danger of death when they decide to leave because abusive relationships are based on control. When she leaves, his control is lost. That's why places like HAWC (Houston Area Women's Center) and AVDA (Aid to Victims of Domestic Abuse) and other nationally recognized DV experts suggest carefully planned exit strategies when leaving. [Note: this is another book for another day]. So actually, it's not as easy as it seems to just leave. "We", victims, do actually try and leave, it just doesn't always work out as we plan.

Oh snap, I'd slipped and made it personal. I'd accidentally let them know that I'd been abused. So, then I made sure I spoke as if it was in the past. I was careful not to tell them that I was still in the relationship. It somehow seemed better, after accidently outing my abuse, to act like it was in the past. In any case, now they knew. So, I continued

I was in an abusive relationship. If you think I wasn't ashamed; I was. I was ashamed because I am a high achiever. I've always been able to fix everyone else's problems; to be in control of all aspects of my life. Before that relationship, I'd always said I would never allow a man to put his hands on me. Yet there I was. I couldn't get a handle on it. I'd tried to leave on multiple occasions and he always knew just what to say or do to convince me to give us one more try. He'd try yelling. If that didn't work, he'd be kind, caring and considerate. He'd make promises to fix all the things I complained of in our relationship. He'd buy flowers. He'd romance me. He'd tell me he couldn't live without me. He'd say we were meant to be together: God ordained it. He promised it would be better. I wanted to believe him because I loved him. I had a child with him, my only child. I wanted a man to love me. He said he loved me. My Dad's suicide and having no father or father-figure in my young life had something to do with that issue. I was clingy and needy. I didn't want to be a single parent like my mother. I wanted my son to have both of his parents together. I knew I deserved to be treated better. And he constantly promised to do so. It was easier to believe in his promises than face the negative judgment of everybody else or the struggles of single parenthood.

Besides that, he didn't start out abusing me. If he had, I wouldn't have fallen in love with him in the first place. Abusive men don't start out hitting and yelling at you. He started out playing pretend. He pretended to be my prince charming. He'd asked me what I wanted in a man. I told him. He became that man, my ideal man, until I fell in love. Then he showed his true self: my abuser and tormentor.

I explained to them that neither socio-economic status, race, culture nor creed matters in an abusive relationship. Welfare recipients, socialites, professional women, etc. can be abused. In some cases, the more prominent you are, the more reasons you had to hide the shame associated with your abuse. In my case, I was somewhat of a public figure and people knew me as strong so to have my abuse be outed was not an option, so I stayed. When we get black eyes, or our hair pulled out or other injuries, we generally try to hide our abuse. We try to explain away our bruises with non-abuse explanations. To explain away him pulling out my hair, I would explain that receding hairlines run in my family. We either make up excuses not related to our abusers, or we just don't go out in public. Makeup is a good tool used for covering up bruises, so is clothing. We don't want to run into anyone we know because inevitably they'll ask us questions and our abusers will think something is going on even when it's not. You find abused women looking down all the time, to avoid eye contact. It's easier to just be invisible than have to deal with the abuse that will likely result from interactions with others.

Abusers constantly break down any self-esteem you have. They constantly ridicule you. I remember one New Year's we were living in Spain. I got dressed up and put on my make-up. I wanted to be pretty for him. I loved him. We went out to celebrate the holiday. He said, "You know Baby, I love you, but the way you put your make-up on today was ugly. I've seen you look better". I was hurt. When I was pregnant with our child, he told me I was fat and ugly. He told me I was stupid. He told me no man would want me because I wasn't a virgin and I had a child. He told me I was used goods. I believed all that he said because he was the one person who I loved most in the world. I didn't think I could do better because he had caused me to isolate myself from my support group, so I heard nothing positive about myself. When I did, on rare occasions, try and reach out for help, my family and friends, the ones I told about it, called me stupid or made comments like, "Girl, you should've left him a long time ago. If I were you, I would have." Or they would say, "What's wrong with you, are you stupid?" At some point, you get tired of hearing other people tell you something's wrong with you. You feel stupid and ashamed. So, you just stop telling them and you keep hoping that he will eventually keep his promises.

I went on and on about this subject to them. The discussion went on through lunch. They seemed to have a better understanding of the cycle of abuse and then started to blame who they should have blamed in the first place: the abuser. Ironically, at the time I had this discussion with my colleagues, I'd tried and failed to leave my ex too many times to count. As a matter of fact, I was actually speaking with them during one of my failed break-ups. Notwithstanding this insightful conversation with them, I ended up allowing him to talk his way back into my life and our relationship went on for another year before I finally left him.

Let's go back to the beginning. How did I become a victim of domestic abuse and violence? In 1990, I was the defending US Heptathlon Champion. I'd already had a Jolanda Jones Day, in the City of Houston, had graduated from UH Magna Cum Laude, with a Political Science Degree, was voted the UH Most Outstanding Senior Award by faculty, had earned multiple Dean's List Semesters, and multiple Academic All-American Awards. I'd earned an unprecedented NCAA Top Six Award, three NCAA Heptathlon Championships, and earned placement on multiple US Track and Field teams, among other accomplishments but something was missing. I didn't have someone to share my very accomplished life with. In my mind, that's all I was missing.

We met in the UH athletic weight room. He was extremely handsome and spoke Spanish. I spoke Spanish too. It wasn't my native language, but I could tell it was his. ¡Qué romantico! I learned he was Colombian, stood 7'1" and played basketball for UH. He was an athletic specimen with my ideal body type. He was flat out fine! He begged me to go out with him for a month before I agreed to a date. He swept me off of my feet on our first date. He took me to salsa dance and I love dancing. I caught on quick. He was so tall that he had to duck to enter doorways. He's how I learned that standard doorways were 7'. Notwithstanding his height, he was as coordinated as any 6'2" man. I thought he'd be goofy like most tall people I knew. I learned that he'd grown up playing soccer, just like Hakeem Olajuwon. He'd been a goalie and had fantastic footwork. It showed on the dance floor. I was pleasantly surprised. I thought I wasn't going to like him, but he appeared to be what I was waiting for, my Prince Charming.

Later that week, on the weekend, our next date was in Galveston, at a Colombian festival. I wore a thong bikini. I always wore thongs. It wasn't something I thought about. Some random guy screamed to me that I should compete in the bikini contest. That I would win. Alejandro accused me of doing something to get that guy's attention. I must've looked at the guy the wrong way. I hadn't. I tried to explain that some men are disrespectful of women, even when the women are clearly with another man. I was used to cat calls, so I just asked

Alejandro to ignore him. That wasn't to be. Alejandro's mood changed. He was pissed. He refused to speak to or with me even though I tried to speak with him. We ended up leaving early. The drive back to Houston was long, quiet and uncomfortable. He blamed me for what happened in Galveston. That was the first sign of his controlling nature. It was within our first week of dating. I should've paid attention. When he showed me who he was, I should've believed him. I should've left. I didn't.

I began noticing Alejandro's jealousy but didn't think much about it. I just thought it meant he loved me. I thought he'd get used to the attention I got but would understand that he should ignore it, just like I ignored the attention he got from women; that I was dedicated to him; that I loved him. I mistook his jealousy for love. I'd been waiting for love. Now I thought I had it.

Here's some of the unapologetic, uncut and unafraid truth. Rosemary saw Alejandro hit me within a month of us dating. He wanted us to go out to the hottest club in town, Yucatán Liquor Stand. I invited Rosemary to come with us. Alejandro picked us up and we went. The place was crowded. Elbow to elbow. Standing room only. We were enjoying the ambiance. Alejandro had to go to the restroom. He went. As soon as he left, two men approached our table and started trying to holler at me. By then, I knew Alejandro was the jealous type, so I did what I could do to try and get the guys to leave before he returned from the restroom. I knew he'd blame me for their actions and I just didn't want to have to deal with it. I didn't feel like arguing over something that wasn't my fault. I flat out asked the guys to move on. I told them that I wasn't interested. They weren't trying to hear it.

I then told them I had a boyfriend. They didn't believe that either. They asked that if I really had a boyfriend, then why would he leave me all alone? I explained that he went to the restroom and that he was coming back. They thought I was lying, so they went on to asked me what he looked like. I said he was 7'1". They laughed and said, "yeah, right." They still didn't believe me. Then here comes Alejandro, walking back to the table. I frantically turned to them and tried to get them to hurry up and leave, please! I must've had a scared look on my face because, the next thing you know, they were looking into the direction that I'd been looking. They must've seen Alejandro because they took off scurrying like roaches when you turn the lights on, away from our table. I prayed that Alejandro hadn't seen them.

My prayers went unanswered. Alejandro had in fact seen them and was so angry that he hauled off and slapped me on the side of my face, in front of Rosemary and anyone in the club who was looking. He hit me so hard that my earring flew out of my ear. It was my favorite pair. I scrambled on the floor to try to find my earring but couldn't. I was trying to make things look perfect. I was trying to figure out what just happened. It didn't make sense. He yelled at me about cheating on him. He said I was such a whore that I couldn't even respect him enough to not publicly try to pick up some guy while he went to use the restroom. He said I was disrespectful. I was in shock. I tried not to cry. I was so embarrassed. He'd never hit me before. He'd only been physically intimidating and had gotten into my personal space. There were times when he'd seemed angry enough to hit me, but he didn't. In the past, he'd pushed me and yelled at me. He berated me, but he'd never actually hit me. This night, he let his anger show in public. He continued to yell after he hit me in the face. He was screaming that I was a cheater, as he stormed out of the club.

Rosemary and I chased after him trying to calm him down and trying to explain that I didn't do anything; that I was trying to make those guys leave, and that I'd told them that I was taken; that he was my boyfriend; that I loved him. He didn't believe us. He'd parked across the street. He jumped into his Ford Bronco, it was Black and tan, and oh, by the way, his agent had gotten it for him against NCAA rules, but Rosemary and I tried to jump into the Bronco, before he left. He would only allow Rosemary in; not me. Then he sped off. There I was, standing in the parking lot crying and embarrassed; trying to figure out how I was going to get home. By the grace of God, Rosemary was able to eventually get him to turn around and come back and get me and allow me into his Bronco. All he did was berate me, in Rosemary's presence, on the ride back. I was so ashamed. It's interesting that I worried more about what Rosemary thought than about the violence he'd just committed against me full-frontal, in front of the whole world to see. I was afraid for what would happen when we got home and how I could explain away what had just happened. We got back to UH and dropped Rosemary off. Sometime later Rosemary re-urged me to leave Alejandro. Even after he hit me in front of her, I still didn't take her advice.

In any case, after we dropped off Rosemary, I got beat that night for my perceived transgressions. I tried to break up with him. I explained that I wouldn't allow him to beat me and that I'd never been in a relationship with violence. Although I loved him, I couldn't be in an abusive relationship. And that his jealousy was unacceptable. He apologized. He cried. I was surprised. It's like he flipped the switch. He went from extreme anger to great sorrow for his bad behavior. He explained that he'd never hit a girlfriend before but that he just loved me so much that he couldn't help himself. That he didn't realize what he was doing. He promised me that he would never hit me again. He also begged me not to leave him. He promised to do better. I believed him. I stayed.

I'd created the beginnings of a love story in my mind. When I met him, it was March 1990. He'd transferred from Houston Baptist University where he was a star and starter on the Huskies team. He was forced to leave HBU because the basketball team had been shut down due to NCAA violations. Alejandro was highly recruited. He chose the University of Houston. His first season at UH had just ended. He was frustrated because he hadn't played much. He mostly sat the bench. That's why he was in the weight room. I was in the weight room too that day, training to defend my previous year's US Heptathlon Title. He was trying to earn a starting spot by working hard in the off season. Since we'd started dating, of course I supported him. I went to the weight room with him and spotted him with his weightlifting. I went to the gym with him and shagged balls for him. I fed him the ball, so he could work on his moves. He worked hard on his short fade away jumper. He worked on the move that made Hakeem famous ~ the Dream Shake. When I met Alejandro initially, he was humble. He was trying to prove himself. He didn't feel like he'd been given a fair shake his first season at UH. Camilo Huerta was the star of the team and he too was an international player from Venezuela. Alejandro and he became good friends. They had the same agent too.

Alejandro's hard work paid off. When his second UH season started, which was his last year of NCAA eligibility, he was killing it. He was stronger and more polished. He was scoring and rebounding, practically at will. I was so proud of him, especially having been able to help him in the weight room and on the basketball court. He won MVP at a tournament in North Carolina. He almost always made the all-tournament teams at the tournaments. Oh, did I enjoy attending his games! I was, what we call now, a basketball wife, almost. After games, I waited for him, to shower and interview, and come out of the tunnel, just like all of the girlfriends waited for their boyfriends. It seemed like our hard work was paying off. He was projected to go high in the draft: a first-rounder. He was now getting interviewed on the news and he was a big deal on Spanish-language news stations. He was growing into a star. The brighter his star shone, the lazier he got, the bigger his head got, and the more he stayed out, later and later.

Women were reaching out to him all day, every day. He was such a hot commodity that they didn't care that he was dating me. They were bold and went after what they wanted – him. He relished in the attention and ultimately ended up cheating on me repeatedly. If a lady showed the slightest bit of interest, chances were he'd figure out a way to sneak away and cheat with her. Since I wasn't a cheater, it never occurred to me that he was cheating. He broke up with me often. Then shortly thereafter, he'd say he missed me and realized he couldn't live without me. I'd take him back. At some point, I realized that his breakups allowed him to sleep and carry on with other women and not be "technically" cheating. I'd break up with him often, but he'd always talk his way back into my life. When he stayed out all night, I just figured he was hanging out with his friends. I'd smell what appeared to be woman's cologne on his shirt. I'd answered many hang-up phone calls. I'd even found hand-written notes in his clothes pockets when I washed them and one in particular had a lipstick kiss on it. Notwithstanding all of this circumstantial evidence of cheating, he always said that women approached him, but he didn't give them the time of day. He said he'd kept the numbers just to be courteous and not disrespect them by throwing them away in their face or not accepting them, and he'd accidently brought them home. He swore that he was just being polite. That he loved me and would never cheat on me. He always had an excuse to explain away his suspect behavior. I was gullible. I wanted him to be telling me the truth, so I hoped that he was.

The first confirmation that he cheated on me stands out in my mind because it was the first time I knew for sure. I wasn't crazy. He'd broken up with me. It turned out to be for a weekend. We got back together. So, I was back staying in his dorm room when he was away. UH played Baylor, in Waco, that weekend. His phone rang. I answered it like I always did. A lady asked if Alejandro was home and why was I answering his phone. I answered because I was his girlfriend and I could. And furthermore, why was she calling my boyfriend? She said that's not what he'd told her previously. Alejandro had told her that he and I were broken up. Even when I confronted him about the call, his excuse was that we weren't technically together. Yada, yada, yada.

He consistently pressured me to change my life and routine. It wasn't an in-your-face demand. It was more subtle so, for the most part, I stopped going out in public. I stopped training, which required me to go to the track, five days a week. He couldn't understand why I still needed to train. I already had multiple national championships. Now it was his time. He asked me not to defend my national championship if I loved him. We needed to focus on him. To prove my love for him, I retired from track and field as the defending 1989 US Heptathlon Champion. I was 24 years old. Me not going to the track everyday also meant I didn't have to risk seeing people. Nor did I have to explain why I no longer socialized. I'd learned that it was easier for me to avoid people because if I ran into anyone I knew, and I spoke with them, Alejandro would accuse me of cheating; the next thing you know, we're in an argument. I stopped going to family events because he'd always politely make me choose: He'd say, "if you love me, then you'll stay with me. We're my family. I love you." He always had something planned to conflict with my family's events or he was too tired from basketball practice. On a few occasions, when he came with me to my family's, he wouldn't be sociable. I really wanted to attend my ten-year high school reunion. He didn't. I begged him to come. I'd been an ugly duckling in high school who'd gone to prom with my best friend, who felt sorry for me, so I wanted to attend with my boyfriend. Alejandro relented but had a seriously stank attitude about being there. He literally sat at the bar and drank the entire time and never spoke to anyone. It was clear to anyone who observed that he didn't want to be there, and we weren't talking. I should've gone by myself. If I went somewhere without him, he'd call incessantly asking when I was going to be home. It was worth it, for peace of mind and to try to avoid arguments, to just not go out if he didn't want to go.

I had my own apartment. He had his own dorm room. So depending on the day, we'd be at either. I had my first job out of college, working as a Minority Recruiter and Admissions Counselor for the University of Houston. I had $10,000 saved in the bank. I was 24 years old. Once he knew I had money, he immediately let me know he needed things, so I bought them for him. He needed glasses. I bought them. Ironically, I wouldn't spend my savings on me, but I freely spent it on him. I owned a used Volkswagen GTI, with a sun roof. It was paid for; no car note. I was proud of that. He made fun of my car.

He wouldn't ride in it. My feelings were hurt. I thought it was a big deal to be 24 and not have a car note and have money saved in the bank. Whatever he needed, I bought it for him. Eventually, all of my savings were gone. Prior to me depleting my savings for him, I'd shared with him that I was worried about not having a savings. He explained that he loved me and that he was going to be a rich professional basketball player and that he would take care of me. Although I was still nervous because I'd worked so hard to be independent and have money in the bank, to have my own apartment and car, and to not live as an adult as I was forced to live as a child, I believed in our fairytale. He promised that one day I would be his wife. He knew I wanted a family. I'd told him my hopes, dreams and aspirations. He became them. He assuaged all of my concerns and fears about losing my independence. Just like my savings became ours. When he signed his contract, and he promised, it would be ours. I wouldn't have to worry about money. He'd take care of me. I believed him.

I refused to let go of my dreams of Alejandro and I eventually becoming a family notwithstanding that his jealousy continued. His physical and emotional abuse continued too. His apologies after the fact continued. At some point I realized I was pregnant. I'd been training to defend my national championship and I blacked out one day while bench pressing. Thank God I had a spotter. For those of you who don't lift weights, a spotter is someone who is there to help you lift the weight you're lifting if it's too heavy for you to lift by yourself. I didn't know why I black out. I just wrote it off to being dehydrated. I drank more water. Then another day, shortly thereafter, I fainted while standing in line to pay for gasoline. By the grace of God, I just so happened to be standing next to a wall and sort of fell onto the wall and slid down it. When I came to, other people in line helped me get up and helped me to my car. I immediately called Alejandro's and told him what had happened. He said to me, "you're pregnant." I was in disbelief. Not again, I was on birth control pills. I wasn't happy. Our relationship wasn't a healthy one and I didn't want to bring a baby into our messed up situation. I decided to have an abortion and I told Alejandro so.

At that point of our relationship, we were breaking up and getting back together, over and over again. Someone was giving him money under the table, I suspect it was his agent, because all of a sudden, he had wads of cash and was spending money and going out and partying all of the time. My savings were long gone but Alejandro wasn't spending money on me nor did he pay me back my $10,000. So, I was disillusioned with our relationship to say the least. I was tired of him yet here I was, pregnant with his child. Alejandro was being courted by many teams in the NBA but the Philadelphia 76er's had drafted him in the Second Round of the 1991 NBA Draft. Alejandro was livid. How dare they wait until the Second Round to draft him. Initially, he was projected to go high in the First Round. And that's what Alejandro expected. Unfortunately, however, he'd been scoring and defending less, in my estimation, because he was no longer focused on basketball. He was more focused on the women and the fame and wasn't practicing as hard. He was partying and drinking a lot. And then he ended up getting hurt, in the NIT Tournament when UH played Stanford. He hadn't rehabilitated as he should have so he'd gained weight, almost 30 pounds, and wasn't as mobile or agile as he'd been before. Besides that, he'd expected a big contract. The 76'ers only offered him the minimum, which was less than $200,000 a year. If my memory serves me well, it was somewhere in the $175,000 range. He showed me the contract and refused to sign it. He was pissed off and insulted. In his mind, he was worth more than that.

Alejandro's best friend Camilo, although drafted by an NBA team, had signed a bigger contract in Spain and played there. So, Alejandro decided to go that route and play overseas in Malaga, Spain, for Unicaja Ronda. They played in the Spanish-equivalent of the NBA, the ACB. He signed a lucrative contract of over $800,000 dollars. He'd negotiated payment to be in cash, tax-free US dollars.

By this time, it was obvious that Alejandro's promises to me that we'd be a family, when I had $10,000 to spend on him, were broken. After I told him I was having an abortion, all of a sudden, he was back to, "we were going to be a family". I didn't believe him. I was still going to have an abortion. He asked if he could come over to my apartment. I said yes. To me it didn't matter. There was nothing he could say to change my mind. When he arrived, he begged me not to abort his child. I wasn't trying to hear him. He'd promised me things before, namely that he wouldn't abuse me or cheat on me, and he always broke his promises. I was resolute in my decision, that is until he called his mom, back in Colombia, long distance. H whined to her that I'd just told him that I was going to abort his child. He emphasized, to her, that he'd even told me that he and I would be a family with the baby. I was shocked, surprised and embarrassed. I couldn't believe he'd just put our personal business out there to his mom without warning me first. And then, without warning, he placed the phone in my hand and wrapped my fingers around it. He told me to explain, to his mom, how I was going to kill our child. I slowly lifted the receiver and explained to his mom about how unhealthy our relationship was. I told her about his cheating on me, but I didn't tell her about his physical violence against me. I don't know why I left that part out. I guess I was ashamed, and I didn't want to make him look worse to his mom. His mom explained to me that now that we were with child, that he would stop the cheating on me. Apart from that, she said, "I was his number one; the woman he came home to; the woman who was carrying his baby." That meant he truly loved me. I relented. I changed my mind. Things would be different now that I was pregnant. He'd told his mom that he wouldn't cheat on me anymore. He'd told his mom that we were going to be a family. He asked me to quit my job at UH and move with him to Spain. I wouldn't have to worry about money. He would take care of our family. He was happy. His mom was happy. We were finally going to be a family and that made me happy. All his previous sins were forgiven. I stayed yet again.

All these years later, that was the ONE request that Alejandro made to me that was 1000% right. Jiovanni is the greatest gift God has ever blessed me with. Needless to say, the violence continued. The cheating continued, and he graduated to raping me. So yes, you can be raped by your boyfriend, intimate partner or spouse.

Now all was well and good with the world. It was like we were on a honeymoon without getting married. We didn't have any problems for a while. He was treating me well. After he signed the contract with Unicaja Ronda, he had a lot of money. He planned on us visiting Colombia, before we officially moved to Spain, so he could see his family and floss his newly acquired success and money. He was smelling himself. You see, in Colombia, Alejandro was famous, the first Colombian drafted in the NBA Draft. When we arrived, the media was waiting on "El Gigante", the Giant. We were in the newspaper, almost every day because he was "el famoso Alejandro", he was famous. We stayed in Cartagena, in a luxury hotel. We were living like rock stars.

Our honeymoon lasted until we landed in Colombia. We couldn't fly directly to Cartagena because, unbeknownst to me, the airport had been blown up. I had no idea who Pablo Escobar was then. Instead we flew to Barranquilla and drove to Cartagena. That was the road trip from hell. The hotel in Cartagena was great, with all of the modern conveniences of the US, but when we finally arrived in Marialabaja, I learned that I had no appreciation of what third world conditions really looked like. The rural conditions exacerbated my problem pregnancy. The homes were nothing like I'd seen in the US. Poor homes in Houston were better than the homes there. Most homes were shacks. Believe it or not, there were homes that were worse than shacks. Those homes were more like huts in that were made of mud and sticks with dirt floors. I remember being shocked that the huts didn't wash away when it rained. I couldn't understand why they swept the dirt floors with a broom. It made no sense to me.

There was no running water or hot water. Alejandro had had a well dug on his family's property for fresh water. It had been dug immediately prior to our arrival. He paid for it with his newfound wealth. No one else in the town, except for the mayor, had their own well. The rest of the village got their water from a river/creek that animals bathed in, fisherman fished in, and women washed clothes in. It was flat out dirty. After the villagers got the water in buckets or whatever they could hold it in, they carried it back to wherever they lived in the village, sometimes up to a mile. There also was no sewer system so people didn't have toilets. Instead most families had an area outside that everyone knew was for using the restroom. There were usually two big flat rocks, to step on, that elevated you while you squatted to use the restroom. In Alejandro's case, he'd paid to have an outhouse with a toilet and make-shift shower installed, in his parent's back yard. Sheets covered the doors for privacy. The toilet didn't flush but if you poured a bucket full of water, from the well into it, and it would drain. No water ran in the shower, so I had to get the cold water from the well, lug it over to the shower stall, pour it over me and bathe in it. I hate cold baths. Alejandro didn't even get the water out of the well and bring it to me. I think they had it better on Little House on the Prairie

The scorching heat was debilitating and making me sicker and sicker. I had to sit outside because at least there was a breeze. There was no air conditioning or electricity. Alejandro had paid to rent in a generator to provide electricity for fans he'd purchased. To compensate for there not being any central air, I was taught to wet a sheet, put it on me, and turned on the fan in my direction, which was powered by the generator. It wasn't an air conditioner, but it was definitely better than nothing. It cooled the wet sheet which consequently cooled me, until the sheet dried. Then I was hot again. Then I repeated the process.

There were mosquitoes everywhere, so I slept in a mosquito net with the fan cooling the wet sheet. Between the living conditions, the heat, nausea, and migraines, I was miserable. I'd been begging Alejandro to take me be back to Cartagena. He wouldn't, and he told me to stop complaining.

That evening, imagine my surprise when I saw a man on a donkey, riding down the street with a cow attached via a rope. The man rode the donkey right into Alejandro's parents' yard and tied the cow to a tree. I was like, "what the hell?" I learned that since there was no refrigeration, Alejandro had to buy a live cow to have a fresh feast. I was told that the women were going to prepare the cow the next day for the feast. I was in shock. The next morning, after a rough night's sleep, I awoke to find cow parts laying all over the ground on banana tree leaves. I was nauseous. I had just seen the cow walking and mooing the previous day. Now it was all cut up. I tried to eat the beef stew, made with the cow. It tasted funny. I couldn't hold it down. I threw up. My head was killing me, and the smell of the stew made me nauseous. As time passed, I grew hungrier and sicker.

I tossed and turned all night and woke up at the crack of dawn. Again, I begged Alejandro to please take me back to the hotel. Again, he refused. His mom saw me crying and throwing up. We'd been in Marialabaja for a couple of days. Thankfully, she suggested that he take me back. He relented but he was pissed. He had a hangover. He expected me to drive since it was me who wanted to go back, but I couldn't. I was still throwing up and had a migraine. Besides that, I didn't know how to get back to Cartagena. The roads weren't paved and there were potholes everywhere. People, animals and carts were along the road. Begrudgingly, he drove. He was extremely irritated. Surprisingly and thankfully, I was able to fall asleep in the car, probably because there was air conditioning. Although it was a bumpy ride, I was more comfortable than I'd been in a couple days.

The next thing I knew, I'm was awakened by a jolt. Alejandro had hit something. The car screeched to a halt. I open my eyes and a man was flying in the air, his body flailing. He landed with a thud. Alejandro had hit an elderly man and his wooden cart that carried plantains. The man was bleeding, moaning and groaning in the middle of the street. He was clearly in pain and injured. The cart was destroyed, and plantains were strewn everywhere. We jumped out of the car to see how he was. Alejandro was yelling at me telling me that it was my fault that he hit the man; that if I had just driven, in the first place, then the wreck wouldn't have happened. We tried to call for an ambulance but there were none, so we picked the man up from the ground, carried him to the car, and drove him to the nearest hospital. It seemed like it took us at least an hour to get him there. The conditions were deplorable. They placed the man on a metal gurney, while he waited to be seen. He was moaning and crying with no pain medication. He was waiting for hours. I stood by his side when I wasn't trying to get the hospital staff to attend to him. Laying right next to him, on another gurney, was a corpse. I was creeped out, plus I was still sick and getting hungrier and weaker every second. No one cleaned up the dried blood on the man. It was just flat out nasty. Like Marialabaja, there was no air conditioning or closed windows, so flies were everywhere.

I wanted to wait to see if the man lived and to know what his diagnosis was, but it took them forever and I wasn't feeling any better. Before we left, I asked Alejandro if we could please come back to see how the man was doing. He didn't commit to anything. So, we left. Later, I finally convinced Alejandro to bring us back to the hospital. When we came back, we learned that the man had lived, thank God, but that he had numerous broken bones, collapsed lungs and other injuries. While there I noticed that blood was backed up into the man's IV. I didn't think that was normal, so I reported it to the hospital, and they promised that they would unclog it, although they didn't do it before we left that day. We found out that Alejandro had destroyed the man's livelihood, his cart and his inventory, the plantains. His body and health were messed up too. He was going to be in rehabilitation for months, at least six. I remember thinking that the quality of healthcare was so bad that if I ever had an emergency in Colombia, I would rather die trying to get back to the US than be treated there.

When the man was released from the hospital, I begged Alejandro to go visit him, so we did. The man lived in a small shack, with no modern conveniences. He was obviously poor. I felt horrible about how we took his livelihood from him because of Alejandro's actions. During the visit, I whispered to Alejandro how I thought he should give the man at least $10,000. He'd just signed that huge contract and was spending money like it grew on trees. I actually hoped he'd give him $25,000, which would probably hold him over for a year until he healed, but I knew Alejandro would never go for that. Alejandro was angry at me for talking about HIS money, especially in the presence of the man. He whispered back to me to shut up. All of my discussions with him were in English. The man was from a small village and it was obvious that he had little education, if any. I didn't even think he read and wrote Spanish, so there wasn't a snow ball's chance in hell, that he spoke or understood English. And I'd chosen English for that very reason. I reminded Alejandro that the man only spoke Spanish. Eventually Alejandro agreed to give the man $5,000, only because he thought that if the man ever figured out who he was, "El Gigante", that we could argue that they agreed to that amount to settle any lawsuits; otherwise, I'm certain he wouldn't have given him anything. I remember thinking that Alejandro's payment to that man was always about covering Alejandro's behind, and never about making right what he'd done wrong. When we got back in the car to leave, Alejandro continued to yell at me, for in his words, not being "loyal" to him. He said I defended the man over him and that was wrong. Unexpectedly he punched me in my pregnant stomach and threatened that I should never side with someone over him again and that I should shut up and let him be the man. I was afraid to speak after that. The ride back to Cartagena seemed like an eternity. I was petrified for myself and for our unborn son.

From Colombia, we flew to Spain. I was very pregnant, almost seven months. It started off well enough. Alejandro was one of two foreigners on Unicaja. The foreigners were the best paid players on each team ~ the Stars. He was treated like a king. We were housed in a three-story condo built into a mountain overlooking the Mediterranean. The floors were marble, and the door knobs and faucets were gold. Everywhere we went, throngs of people surrounded Alejandro. They loved him. In the European leagues there were super high expectations for the two foreigners, that's why they got paid so much more money than the native players. They expected the foreigners to carry the team to a championship. When Alejandro was playing in European leagues, players like Croatian Toni Kukoc and Lithuanian Arvydas Sabonis were super starring over there. That's how they both ended up in the NBA. That's what Unicaja Ronda expected from Alejandro. Alejandro expected to dominate in the ACB and use that as a stepping stone to return to the NBA with a multimillion-dollar contract. He was supposed to carry his team into the European Championships. His over $800,000 US cash tax-free salary was paid prorated. If I remember correctly, it was to be paid over eight months, so he got paid over $100,000 per month in brown paper bags, in cash US dollars. I remember the first time I saw a month's installment laying on the bed, after Alejandro, dumped it out of the bag. I almost fell out. I couldn't believe it. All I could do was look but not touch. Me sharing and ultimately spending all of my savings on him was not reciprocated by him. I had more money with my $10,000 savings than I ever had when I was with him. What he didn't spend, he deposited it in the bank, Unicaja Ronda, which was the title sponsor of his team. He was balling shot calling. I was poor and was forced to watch his excessive life style. It was so oxymoronic.

The pressure was enormous. The fans loved you one minute and if you faltered or the team started losing, they were throwing beer cans at you and chanting nasty things about you the next minute. It was no different for Alejandro. As the latest foreign star, the women were everywhere trying to get them some Alejandro and there I was pregnant. Since I didn't start showing until I was seven months, I didn't really look as pregnant as I was. I was still agile and exercising. Even though we were in a Spain, I felt comfortable and besides that, I spoke the language. I knew that so long as Alejandro worked hard and was disciplined, no one would be better than him. He had to go to practice. That was his job. I went with him. I was his biggest supporter and cheerleader. When I wasn't helping him by shagging balls after practice, I played basketball. After all, I had been a high school All-American basketball player myself. They were so surprised at my athletic ability and basketball skills, even at seven months pregnant, they offered me a contract, to play for the women's team, paying approximately $70,000, per year after Jio was born. Alejandro didn't like the attention I was getting so he stopped bringing me to practice and he wouldn't let me accept the contract. He clearly wanted to be the only star in the family. I was okay with that. I wanted to support him and not threaten him, so I intentionally tried to dim my light. I made an effort to blend in and be as helpful as I could to him. I cooked his meals so that when he came home his food was on the table. I was the dutiful girlfriend.

Alejandro's happiness seemed to wane. His star was dimming quickly. When the season started, I loved attending his games. I was proud of him from coming up from poverty. He was finally treating me nice. The highlight of my days were attending his games and cheering him on. He was working out and coming home to me at night. I thought we were on a right path finally. Then he started complaining about having to practice; he didn't believe that he should have to practice twice a day. He complained of having a hard life. All I could think about was how ungrateful he was; getting paid close to $1 million dollars a year and having to work out twice a day and play games and "you're bitching". I knew better than to say it.

He started coming home later and later; and sometimes not coming home until in the morning.

Since he was so irritable, I tried to stay out of his way. Therefore, I befriended the wives and girlfriends of his teammates. I tried to stay in my lane. They appreciated that I spoke the language and embraced their culture. They said I wasn't arrogant like most Americans. Since there was socialized healthcare for everyone, regardless of citizenship, I immediately started going to prenatal checkups and Lamaze classes. They were free. I wanted my delivery to go more smoothly than my pregnancy. Alejandro didn't want to go to my check-ups with me, so I went with my best girlfriend, whose name sadly, I can no longer remember. For purposes of this book, I'll call her Amelia. Alejandro also didn't want to attend Lamaze classes, so Amelia attended those with me too. To get her to attend Lamaze classes with me, I explained that Alejandro was too tired from practice to attend. She said she understood. Surprisingly he had no problems with her being my Lamaze partner. Although I was disappointed that he wouldn't attend with me, I was hopeful that when Jiovanni was born that Alejandro would come around.

At some point, Alejandro forbade me from attending his practices and games. The excuse he gave was that I got too excited and he was concerned I was going to induce labor and somehow do harm to Jio. I was heartbroken. Although naïve, I thought Alejandro didn't understand that pregnant women weren't handicap. I tried to explain that I wasn't disabled, just pregnant. He stood his ground. I felt lonely and isolated. I was all alone almost all day every day. I longed to go home, back to the US. I wanted somebody to talk to, but I wasn't allowed to call home. I grew depressed.

He also banished me to from his bed. I was made to sleep in another bedroom. He wouldn't touch me nor have sex with me. There was no intimacy. He called me fat. I cried a lot and I knew it had more to do with than just hormones. His excuse, for his banishment, was that he didn't want to accidently kick me or hurt me during his sleep. Again, I wrote it off to him having prehistoric beliefs about women. I tried to explain otherwise but I couldn't change his mind. I was going crazy; having a nervous breakdown.

I didn't want anyone to know about our problems, but I needed help convincing Alejandro that I wasn't fragile and to please let me come back to practices and games. I was about to lose my mind. So, I got up the courage to speak with Amelia since I was allowed to speak with her and not get in trouble for it. Besides that, I trusted her, so when Alejandro forbade me from attending his games, I reached out to her for help.

I hadn't intended on telling her everything. When I called her, I lamented about how old fashioned Alejandro was and how he didn't appreciate the strength of women; how he stopped me from coming to games and moved me to another bedroom because he was afraid that somehow the baby might get hurt. I wanted to know if she might speak with her fiancé and have him suggest to Alejandro that I be allowed to come back to his games; to explain to Alejandro that allowing me to sleep in the same bed wasn't dangerous to the baby. There was silence on her end. She finally exhaled, so much so that I heard it, and told me that Alejandro's not allowing me to come to the games had nothing to do with my pregnancy. She said that he was bringing a new girl to the games and that her name was Maria. She was a local girl.

What?! Are you kidding me?! He had some girl replace me at his games?! He'd introduced her to his team?! I was pregnant with his child! No wonder he wasn't touching me. No wonder I got banished from his bedroom. No wonder why he didn't allow me to come to his games. No wonder he was either not coming home at night or coming home really late. And to make matters worse, he had the nerve to introduce her to his team and they knew her name. He seriously tried to replace me. The only good news that she said was that the team and his teammates were livid. They loved and respected me. Everyone was disappointed with him. They were all outdone by his blatant disrespect of me. They could see I was devoted pregnant girlfriend. I asked her why she was just telling me. She said everyone was trying to protect me. They were worried about my psychological well-being. They didn't want to upset me. They didn't know if I knew. Alejandro had told them I was struggling through the pregnancy. Yeah, because of him! They didn't want to negatively affect my pregnancy. The only reason she told me was because I called her. No wonder he was so irritable. She told me that he had been playing horribly; that he was showing up for practice either late or not rested. The team paid too much money to him for him not to be producing. No one liked Maria, but they loved me. For that, I was grateful.

That explained it. Once we were in the grocery store and people chanted, "Juan Valdez!" They were taunting Alejandro; making fun of him. Juan Valdez was the moniker of a popular brand of Colombian coffee. He went from being called "El Gigante" to "Juan Valdez." I remember chuckling when I heard it because I thought it was so funny. He wasn't pleased that I found humor in it. He took my laughter as an act of treason against him. She told me that at the games, the fans would throw things from the bleachers at him. I was surprised but, in my heart, I was smiling. That's what he got for being a liar and cheater. God don't like ugly. What goes around comes around. Karma is a bitch. Interestingly, they were equal opportunity in their criticism of the players. The other foreigner on the team was Valeri Tikhonenko. He wasn't playing up to snuff either, so the fans called him "Paralíticonenko." It rhymed and translated into "Paralytic Tikhonenko". I thought that was funny too. Notwithstanding the humor, the fans were brutal. They loved you one minute and hated you the next.

When he came home that day, I finally asked him about Maria. Who was she? What did I do to him to make him go to her? Where'd he meet her? How long had he been with her? He denied Maria. He denied that she was at games. When I told him I knew everything, he finally admitted it. He went from denying to humiliating me. He told me it was my fault. That if I gave him everything, he needed then he wouldn't need to find someone else. He said she catered to his every need. To make matters worse, he told me I still couldn't come to his games and was still relegated to the other bedroom. He was remained bold and unapologetic about his actions. He was a grown ass man and he was so mad at me that he just couldn't be in the same house as me. So, he stormed out and left.

I was lonely. Crying. Feeling sorry for myself. Depressed. Embarrassed. And, I couldn't call home. He wasn't changing his behavior. So, I thought about ending it all. I was in my eight month of pregnancy. Jio was viable outside of my womb. I'd seen his heart beat. I'd seen him moving. In the States, all I'd been shown was ultrasound pictures. In Spain, they were more medically advanced. I'd seen ultrasound video. If I took pills, would I kill him too? I didn't want to kill Jio. I just wanted to kill myself. What if I killed myself and he lived? Would he be mad at me? Would he be brain damaged? Would he have special needs? Would Alejandro raise my child without me? Would he feel responsible for my death? Would he blame himself? Would Jio have issues related to being the son of suicide? And then I remembered me, and my dad's suicide's effect on me. I would never do to my son what my dad did to me. I would stay alive and protect him and love him like I wished my dad had done for me. Jio was a gift to me from God. He needed me. I didn't want to leave him in anyone's caring arms but mine. That was that. I wasn't going to harm myself or my son. That was one of the last times I contemplated suicide.

One day I was in the kitchen cooking. Alejandro came home angry because his manager, Jacinto, had called him and told him that the team was reevaluating his contract. They were disappointed that he wasn't playing well and attributed it to his philandering ways. Jacinto believed it was me who told the team about his cheating and that my putting his business out to his team was jeopardizing his contract. Of course, he blamed me for something that I didn't do. It was par for the course. I hadn't told anyone. The only person that I'd spoken to about him was Amelia and she actually told me about his cheating, and I'd sworn her to secrecy about the depths of our problems.

Hell, I was embarrassed and ashamed. I reminded him that he took Maria to games and not me. That's how they knew. It was him not me who was interfering with his ability to earn a living. He was angry that the team favored me over him. To him, they didn't realize how difficult a girlfriend I was. They'd given him an ultimatum to leave that girl alone, stop partying all night and re-focus on basketball or else he wouldn't have a job with them. He must've taken what they said seriously because all of a sudden, he was coming home at night, although I still had to sleep in another room. He wasn't talking to me but at least he was there.

We lived in a gated condo so the only way for someone to get in was to call us on the intercom and we had to buzz them in. One day Alejandro and I were both at home and I was in my ninth month of pregnancy. The intercom buzzed. I answered it. It was a woman I didn't know. A female asked to speak with Alejandro. I asked who it was. She wouldn't tell me. I figured that it must be Maria. Alejandro came over to the intercom and basically took over the conversation. He told her that it was over between them and that she couldn't come up. He also said that he wasn't going to come out to see or speak with her. She was begging him. He didn't listen and hung up. She called back a number of times. Alejandro didn't answer. So, he really did stop seeing her. He obviously loved his job more than her. Although I took some solace that he dropped her like a hot potato, his behavior didn't change towards me. He was still isolating and verbally abusive. The physical abuse had slowed. I was at least thankful for that.

About a month before my due date, I felt contractions. Oh no, I was going into labor. The contractions hurt but were bearable. I yelled for Alejandro. He took me to the hospital. As it turns out, I wasn't really in labor. They were Braxton-Hicks contractions. False labor. The hospital sent us home. Alejandro was mad. He said I was too stupid to not even know that I was not in labor. I made him waste his time. I better not call him again unless I was really in labor. I didn't understand why he was so mad at me. I truly thought I was in labor. I was having contractions, at regular intervals, just like they explained to me at Lamaze classes. And, it hurt like hell.

So, the next time I started having pains in regular intervals, which was about two weeks later, I didn't tell Alejandro. I was afraid. I didn't want to be wrong again and make him mad at me. I was in my bed in my bedroom. Alone. Even though the contractions hurt, I was afraid to tell him. I laid there, just trying to get through the pain without making noise and waking him up. Every time I had an urge to scream, I just covered my mouth and tried to muffle any sound that, without my permission, came out of my mouth. The contractions lasted for three hours, and were getting closer and closer together, and were becoming more severe. After hours of suffering in silence and alone, I finally decided that this must be it, I was really in labor. I went to Alejandro's room and told him that I needed to go to the hospital. It was the middle of the night. He was irritated that I woke him up. He didn't believe me. He said he wasn't making a blank trip to the hospital again. He told me to call a taxi and went back to sleep. I didn't want to take a taxi, so I called Amelia. She got up and rushed and came and picked me up about 1am and took me to the hospital. I was in physical pain but emotionally heart broken. Alejandro wouldn't even take me to the hospital, when I was really in labor, and I was delivering his child.

When we arrived at the hospital, the doctor advised me of what I already knew, I was in full-fledged labor, but I hadn't dilated very much so it'd be a while before I delivered Jio. They put me in a room to wait until I was ready to deliver. Amelia said she'd stay with me until Alejandro arrived. Since Alejandro hadn't come to Lamaze classes, he didn't know what to do to help anyway. Truth be told, I was thankful that she was there for me. I knew she'd be nice and kind and besides that, she'd already been coached about how to help me in Lamaze class. I called Alejandro and told him that I'd been admitted and that the doctor told me that I was actually in labor. He said okay, but that he was going back to sleep, and to call him when Jio was born. He had practice in a few hours. I was devastated. I didn't tell Amelia everything Alejandro said, but I did tell her that he couldn't come right now. It didn't matter. She was there for me. She didn't ask any questions. She just coached me through my labor. Every time a contraction would rear its ugly head, she would coach, "Respira, respira" and hold my hand, just like they taught us in class. She was telling me, "breathe, breathe." She would say it in a matter of fact tone and rub my head gently to calm me down. She also reminded me to "Relájate," which meant "just relax". They taught us that, too, in class. She was who I needed with me. She explained so soothingly, with each contraction, that both Jio and I were going to be fine. She stayed up and at my side, calming me as best as she could, the entire time she was there. The pain was so great, that every time a contraction would happen, I just knew I was going to die. I also gasped and held my breathe but she always got me through it with the right words and actions.

Then surprisingly Alejandro showed up. He didn't call or warn me. He ordered her to leave and told me that he was going to be there with me. On the one hand, I was happy that he came, but on the other hand, she knew what to do with each contraction and I trusted her. Before she left, she told Alejandro to remind me to breathe and relax and rub my head or hold my hand to help me. He said okay, we hugged each other, I thanked her, and she left. Alejandro was holding my hand before she left. After she left, he let my hand go and began complaining that there was nowhere for him to sleep. I don't remember if he laid on the chair in my room, or if he asked for a cot, but I do remember that with every contraction, he screamed from the foot of the bed, "breathe, breathe." That was it. No hand holding. No soothing words. No rubbing my head or anything. He was clearly mad that he was there. I couldn't figure out why he came if he was going to act like this. Then I figured it out. He couldn't not be there with me, during labor and the birth of our child. My friend was the fiancé of his teammate. She would tell people, so he came there just to look like he actually cared. I wished he would have stayed home. I went into labor about 10pm. She was with me until about 5am.

Then he came, and my labor got that much harder and the pain seemed to get worse and worse. I begged for an epidural, but I wasn't dilating so they couldn't give me anything for the pain. Alejandro just wanted me to shut up, but I couldn't. It hurt so much. There were discussions with the doctor about doing a C-section. I didn't want a C-section. We waited. The contractions continued getting closer and stronger. I hurt excruciatingly. Alejandro wasn't helpful. Finally, the doctors suggested that I try and push myself into adequate dilation. It was nearly 1pm. If that didn't work, then they were going to take Jio via C-section. I didn't want a scar. I can laugh now but I was worried about having a scar. I wanted to still wear bikinis after my pregnancy. I pushed twice and Jio was out. The doctors said they had never seen such strong abdominal muscles. They were about to lay Jio on my stomach, but Alejandro convinced them to give Jio to him. I was devastated. I just knew the first parental touch Jio was going to have was with me. I felt so empty, pun intended, when Alejandro took Jio. They finally brought Jio to me and put him in my arms. I never felt more love for anything in my life like I felt for Jio at that moment. He was perfect.

The perfection ended about five minutes after Jio was born. Alejandro learned that he was cut from the team. The team didn't want to upset me during my pregnancy so unbeknownst to me, they'd decided to wait until Jio was born to fire him. What should have been the happiest moment, of my life, wasn't. Alejandro was angry. I was just happy to be a mom and that I had a healthy son. I stayed in the hospital for another day and then we went home. Once home, we learned that we had to move out of our beautiful condo. The next foreigner had been signed, Ralph Sampson, would be moving into our digs. I guess it wasn't technically our digs, it was the team's digs. I actually showed Ralph Sampson the condo, we lived in and that he would soon be moving into, like a real estate agent. He was even taller than Alejandro and he walked with a pronounced limp. He was very polite. I was a couple of days out of the hospital and we had less than a week to GET OUT. Alejandro was frantically trying to find us a place to stay because we couldn't fly back home to the States. Babies aren't allowed to fly the first month of their life, especially a transatlantic trip. We also had the little problem of travel documents for Jio. I'd already looked into it, prior to his birth, and had booked an appointment at the US Embassy to get Jio a passport. I got him a passport and noticed, after we finally got back to the US, that in his passport picture, Jio had a little booger in his nose. Lord, have mercy, all I had to do as a mom was wash my child's face and clean his nose, and I couldn't do that right. From his birth until the expiration of his passport, I had a reminder of that booger. I shook my head every time I saw it.

When we moved out of the condo, less than a week after Jio was born, Alejandro found us a flea bag motel to stay in for that month we had to wait to leave Spain. It had a double bed and not much else. I couldn't figure out why we were living in such a deplorable condition, but Alejandro didn't want to spend his money. He liked spending other people's money lavishly but didn't' want to spend his money on me, is the conclusion I reached, over time. Before we left for the US, the team had grown tired of Ralph Sampson, too. If my memory serves me correctly, he was fired before we left. I wondered if he showed the digs to his replacement, like I did for him. They were calling Ralph Sampson and Rafael Vecina, "Los Rodillos Gemelos", the Twin Knees, a play on words and a parody of the "Twin Towers" of Ralph Sampson and Hakeem Olajuwon. You see, they played no favorites. If you weren't playing like the fans thought you should, then you were fair game. Off we flew back to the US ~ Coach, not First Class. Alejandro wasn't happy. Jio was a month old, the magic age when newborns could fly. It was a long flight and Jio cried sometimes. Alejandro hardly held him or helped me on the flight back with him, but none of that mattered. I was so happy to be headed back home – Houston, Texas, USA. Now I was going to get my life back. I wasn't trapped anymore, or so I thought.

After we arrived back in the US in late January 1992, I tried to pick up where I left off before I met Alejandro and moved to Spain. I'd learn from a UH law professor, who graduated from Stanford Law, and who I'd served on a committee with, that I'd earned a scholarship to Stanford Law School. My plans, before Alejandro, were to attend Stanford Law. Well, Alejandro side-tracked me and after having Jio, I couldn't afford daycare in Palo Alto, California. I had to stay home because I needed the help of family and friends to get through law school with an infant. I immediately applied, was accepted, and enrolled UH Law School for the summer part-time program. I'd earned an NCAA Post Graduate Scholarship that I had to use before it expired. When I started law school, Jio was five months old. Alejandro wasn't much help. He refused to babysit Jio. He said he wouldn't keep Jio alone until he could play basketball with him. Consequently, I used to bring him to class with me. Juggling Jio and law school was difficult, especially because I was in a domestically abusive relationship, but I was bound and determined to graduate. I needed to be employable and a law degree would help.

Law school was a struggle. I did all I could do to get through law school and take care of Jio simultaneously. I'd come home from school and was multi-tasking. I was doing homework and watching Jio. Alejandro was angry that I hadn't cooked so he jumped on me. I called the police and he was arrested. My mom called and asked to speak to him. I told her that he wasn't home. He was in jail. I don't know what I expected her to say but I certainly didn't expect her response. Rather than asking me how I was doing, she asked me what I did to make him beat me. Not OMG, baby are you okay? Do you need me to come over? Is my grandson alright? None of that. I was outdone. I hung up and refused to speak with her for six months. Ironically, I took Alejandro back and spoke with him.

Another time, I came home from law school. Jio was crying and wet in the car seat. I needed to come in and change his wet pamper. Alejandro could care less, he believed I was ten minutes late. Alejandro had times in his head for how long it should take me to do anything, including getting from point A to point B. So, he was convinced that I'd gone and had a quickie sex romp with some man. A 10-minute quickie. The fact that I had Jio with me was irrelevant. I was exhausted, emotionally and physically, as I always was from being a single mom and a law student, so I didn't feel like arguing. Plus, I needed to change Jio. Alejandro insisted on starting a fight. He started out accusing me of cheating. He was sitting at the dining room table drinking beer, all alone. He did that often.

He'd drink a twelve pack every day. As he was yelling at me, I walked past the dining room and into our bedroom. I tried to ignore him. I told him I was tired, and I needed to change Jio's diaper. Alejandro kept arguing at me anyway. My mom had called and wanted to speak with Jio, so I passed him the phone. Jio couldn't really talk but that didn't seem to bother my mom. Jio was sitting on the side of the bed, on the floor, holding the phone to his ear, presumably listening to my mom. Alejandro was incensed that I was ignoring him, so he stormed into the bedroom, all 7'1", 265 pounds of him, muscles and all. I was sitting on the side of the bed taking off my clothes, preparing to study. He started hitting and pushing me, while yelling at me, and the next thing I know, he was on top of me kneeling over me, on the bed, with my legs between his knees.

I was trying to get him from hitting be, I was blocking his blows and begging him to please stop; that I hadn't done anything. Before I knew it, his hands were around my throat squeezing, choking me to death. He'd knocked me onto my back in a laying position. It hurt. I couldn't breathe. I couldn't speak. I couldn't yell for help. I started to black out. By the grace of God, instinctively, I thrust my knee into his testicles. He released his hold on my neck and grabbed his groin area. I gasped for air and screamed, "Momma, call 911!" Remember,

Jio was on the phone with her but Alejandro didn't realize it until I screamed. He immediately jumped off of me and to where Jio was and grabbed the phone from Jio and hung it up.

He started to approach me again, asking me why I screamed to my mom. He was talking to me like he thought I was crazy or something. He was talking in a calm voice as if to deescalate. I wasn't the one screaming and strangling somebody, he was. The phone rang. I grabbed it. I thought it was probably my mom. I was wrong. It was the 911 operator. My mom had called 911 just like I screamed. The operator asked me if I was okay. I answered no. I begged for the police. She asked me not to hang up the phone, so I didn't. I grabbed Jio and hugged him. He was crying. Alejandro had jerked the phone out of his hand. Bless his heart, he had no idea what was going on. He couldn't have been more than a year.

Alejandro seemed confused about what I'd just done. He immediately started trying to convince me that he hadn't really done anything to me. I explained that he'd just tried to kill me by strangling me to death. He denied it. He said that he wasn't trying to hurt me; that he just wanted me to shut up, so he was trying to make me be quiet. I explained that I couldn't breathe and that I almost passed out. That had I not kneed him in the balls, that he would've killed me. The police came and arrested him. It wasn't his first time getting arrested for beating me up. That night, he actually called me collect from jail. My dumbass accepted the call. He proceeded to try and persuade me that he didn't try and hurt me. He begged me not to file charges. He blamed me for his actions. That particular night I wasn't trying to hear it. I was just thankful to be alive. I hung up on him. I wish I would've maintained that resolve. Eventually I would let him talk his way back into my life. I refused to cooperate with the prosecutor and his case ultimately got dismissed. That merry-go-round of abuse repeated itself over and over again. I can't remember the number of times he beat me. I just know that I rarely called the police. I ended up calling the police twice in Fort Bend, once in Harris County and once when we lived in Fort Wayne, Indiana, when he played for the Fort Wayne Fury, in the CBA.

As became his routine, he continued his abuse. When he thought I cheated, he would often force me to lie down on the bed. He'd force his finger into my vagina to see if I had a discharge. He'd hold his finger in the air and examine it in my presence. He'd also smell his finger. His assaults of me were painful and humiliating. God forbid I had a yeast infection, Alejandro never believed it was yeast. He always believed it was semen; evidence he said, that supported his belief that I cheated.

He almost always said I smelled like sex. How do you smell like sex when you didn't have sex and you just got home from law school? If he found me guilty of cheating, which he almost always did, he would, at a minimum verbally abuse me. And often times, physically abuse me. Sometimes he'd force me to have sex with him to prove his power over me or to punish me. He also used his "evidence" of semen, to justify leaving and not coming home. I was paranoid of his cheating accusations, so I constantly checked my panties for discharge or odor. I didn't want to get in trouble so if I had a spot or thought I smelled an odor, then I ran to my OB/GYN to get checked. My doctor would explain over and over that it was normal for women to have discharge and nothing was wrong with me. I was a basket case. Nothing my doctor said ever gave me peace of mind because Alejandro always said I was cheating. I never told my doctor that I was being abused and raped and assaulted by Alejandro.

I could go on and on with the stories of Alejandro's abuse of me but I won't, except to say that the straw that broke the camel's back was when Alejandro jumped on me, for something he thought I did, which I didn't, after we were finally married. The significance of the marriage was that he'd promised me he would never lay a hand his wife. And since we got married in July of 1995, he hadn't laid a hand on me. That night, he jumped on me, his wife, in our apartment with Jio, my sister India and her boyfriend, all present. I had to scream for India to call 911. When he ran to try and stop India from calling 911, I ran outside and hid in a neighbor's apartment. After he went outside looking for me, I sneaked back into our apartment and locked him out. I never let him back in. He was getting bolder with his abuse. He used to at least wait until we were alone to abuse me so people wouldn't know that he yelled at me and beat me up. And, I was less likely to be embarrassed in public. I'd finally had enough. I knew marriage wouldn't protect me or make our relationship better. It was November 8, 1995. After almost six years, I was finally convinced he would never change and if I didn't leave him that he would kill me, get away with it and get custody of Jio just like OJ killed Nicole, got away with it and got custody of Sydney and Justin. For once and for all, I didn't stay.

Alejandro also had messed up beliefs about what it meant to be a father. His abuse didn't just stop with me. He abused Jio as well. He didn't call the abuse, abuse. He believed he was teaching Jio to be tough. To be a man. Once when Jio wanted to eat some hot sauce. I explained, to Jio, that hot sauce was hot. Alejandro explained just the opposite and took a spoon full of hot sauce and put it into Jio's mouth. Jio began screaming and trying to take the hot sauce off of his tongue. Alejandro was laughing. I didn't see anything funny about it. Another time, Alejandro wrapped Jio's entire body in a blanket, turned off the lights and left him in the restroom. Jio was screaming his lungs out. When I explained to Alejandro that what he did to Jio was child abuse, he begged to differ. He said he was teaching Jio to be tough. Jio was terrified of the dark well into his teens.

In owning my S.H.I.T! related to Alejandro, I had to accept that I gave him the road map to trick me and steal my heart. Beware because everything that glitters ain't gold. I learned this the hard way. If you tell an insecure person what you are looking for in a relationship, they'll pretend to be who they know you want until they conquer you. Once they have you, they'll revert to who they really are. Make them pay attention to what makes you happy. Don't tell them. And when they do show you who they truly are, believe them the first time. Don't allow them to make excuses for their bad behavior. And, don't you make excuses for their bad behavior.

With each passing second, hour, day, month and year, after I left Alejandro, I began to learn how strong I was. I learned that Jio was adjusting without his dad being there. He wasn't mad at me for leaving his dad like I'd convinced myself he would do. I was learning to own that I had everything within me to get through whatever S.H.I.T! fell my way. It didn't matter if the S.H.I.T! hit me in the gut and knocked the wind out of me. I just had to catch my breath. And whenever I had doubt, I had to remember what Dear always told me, God wouldn't give me more than I can handle, and that God didn't make mistakes. Everything happens for a reason. She consistently reminded me that God gave me gifts that were unique to me, and that I had to identify and use them and not waste them. I was learning that no matter what happens in life, you must stay the course, even if I had to take a quick detour.

I encounter stuck people every day who have no idea how to move forward. Some well into their fifties and sixties who are stuck from some of the same childhood S.H.I.T! that I encountered. This causes a generational cycle of dysfunction because now you have children who are stuck in S.H.I.T!, who are buried in their parent's S.H.I.T! and who learn how not to deal with S.H.I.T! because that's what they're taught by their parents. Then those same kids grow into stuck adults who then raise stuck children and it goes on and on and on. This generational madness must stop.

My marriage taught me a number of lessons to stop the madness. First, I had to forgive myself for the S.H.I.T! I allowed to happen to me. Then I had to forgive Alejandro so his hold over me could dissipate. I've often heard people say, "You have to forgive and forget." I beg to differ. I say, "forgive and remember." So, when Alejandro inevitably tried to creep back into my life, I didn't forget. Instead I remembered our tortuous relationship and I never went back.

Chapter Eleven
Flip the Script On Your S.H.I.T!

There comes a time in life when you either have to
S.H.I.T! or get off the pot! As much as we desire to remain
constipated in our comfort zones, life is about making choices.
If we don't choose, life will ultimately choose for us. Many of
the things that transpired in my life, were out of my control.
As each bad thing happened to me, I had a "why me?" attitude.
My method was to just try to get through it any way I could,
but never feeling like I could control or stop the madness. For
the longest time that was my game plan. Same day, different
S.H.I.T!! Often times, I'd speak with my grandmother about
why God hated me so much. Why I just couldn't catch a break?
When was I going to be able to control my life and be on the
offensive and not on the defensive?

Over the years, eventually and thankfully, with each
incident I was becoming more aware of the power that dwelt
within me. Though very dim, overtime, my power began to
increase, because I was making a conscious effort to become
stronger. I can't succinctly tell you how I did it. It was a
journey. It was complicated. I can say that it was mind over
matter. Finding support systems. Praying a lot, constantly
repeating what my grandmother Dear told me, "Sweetheart,
God will not give you more than you can handle." Such a cliché
but so true if you authentically believe. I couldn't allow the
matters of my heart, to take out my mind, my future, or my
life. Another cliché you've heard is, "A mind is a terrible thing
to waste." Indeed, it is, and I wasn't about to lose mine. As I
shared with you before, I was a highly recruited star athlete, an
all American in both basketball and track and field, having both
academic and athletic full-ride scholarship offers from
Division 1 and Ivy League universities. I was a member of
numerous organizations like the National Honor Society,

Fellowship of Christian Athletes and Spanish Club. I was honored to have numerous Jolanda Jones Days, in Houston and Galveston. I'd finished law school and passed the bar exam and achieved my goal of becoming a lawyer yet my personal life was sometimes out of control, in total disarray. And no one knew. It was my secret.

I protected that secret with everything I had in me. I was ashamed. I was terrified of people finding out that I wasn't perfect. My S.H.I.T! stank but I covered it up so well by super achieving. Hardly anyone had a clue of my tortured existence, most caused by outside forces, but some caused by me. My biggest obstacle, a lifetime of fighting for my mother's love, attention, affection and approval, was overshadowed by my accomplishments.

I carried myself in a way that others wouldn't believe that I came from an impoverished environment with a father who committed suicide. I was created for the express purpose to positively impact the world. I had to encounter loss, death, abuse, rejection, neglect, abandonment, criticism, hurt and pain so that I could be molded and shaped into a woman who was unapologetic and unafraid. My suffering in silence was not in vain, because I was being called to be a voice for the people.

I've been gifted with the ability to feel the pain of others and to fight for them. Believe me, I know how it feels to not have; therefore, I empathize with people who suffer hardships in life, due to a lack of love and support. I've seen more tragedy in my life than most but, to be honest, I wouldn't change it for the world.

Do I wish my mother would've been different towards me, yes, absolutely but as always, my Grand Mommy helped me own my S.H.I.T! related to my mom so I could continue on my path to success. She helped me to redefine my definition of love and life. She said, "What if your mother never tells you she loves you? Will you allow another human being to have that kind of control over you? Are you going to cry and hurt like this for the rest of your life? It's time to figure out how to love yourself!"

Her simple questions led me to the most profound epiphany regarding how to get over my greatest obstacle. It totally changed my life. She taught me that self-love is essential in sustaining you when others hate on you. Apart from that, she consistently confirmed her love for me, less I forgot that I always had her in my corner. She always said, "I am so glad God gave you to me!" She reminded me that I was a gift from God whenever people treated or thought of me as trash, including myself. If I had the opportunity to speak to all the Lil' Jolanda's, out there, I would assure them "that God doesn't make mistakes," which is another golden nugget I learned from my grandmother. She taught me that if you need help, you must learn to ask for it. It's not a show of weakness. It could very well be a strength. How will people know what you're going through, if you don't share and ask for help if you need it? And while you may believe that your blood family should come to the rescue, maybe they won't. You should be receptive to help that may come or be available from the family you create. Pay attention to who's around you and who really loves you and ask them for help. I can honestly say that God placed great people in my life, at all the right times. I was blessed to find others for all things physical, mental, spiritual, emotional and financial needs that I couldn't get from my mom. But for them, especially my grandmother and my son, I wouldn't be here today.

To this day, I cry every time I see Coach T, Tom Tellez, my coach at UH. He's one of the greatest coaches of all time. He coached numerous world record holders and Olympic gold medalist like Carl Lewis. He has also coached numerous US Track and Field teams. My inability to get through my S.H.I.T! ultimately took a dream from me. It costed me my spot on the US Olympic Track and Field Team and a chance at a gold medal, in the Heptathlon, and perhaps the high jump. That failure is a poignant reminder that not owning your S.H.I.T! can forever change your future. It can cause you to lose opportunities that you can never regain. I will never be on the United States Olympic team, ever! I also regret not playing basketball in college, but I was afraid to stand up for what was right for me. Basketball was and will always be my favorite sport. I wish I would've left my husband sooner and hadn't been so damn needy. I wish! I wish! I wish! These things didn't kill me, they made me stronger. What the enemy meant for bad, God or the universe has used for good. As an advocate for the people, I am dedicated to defending and protecting those who are or have been broken and/or ostracized. Owning your S.H.I.T! may be difficult, but it's doable, especially when you're sick and tired of doing the same old S.H.I.T! and getting the same stinky results.

You must SHIFT YOUR THINKING…Change your mindset! It's ULTIMATELY up to you to FLIP THE SCRIPT on your S.H.I.T! and erase and rewrite the scenes of your life. You can't do this unless you know who you are and the strengths you possess. Without these valuable keys to success you will find yourself in a dysfunctional whirlwind that will never end. I could've very well been so caught up in the dysfunction of my life, my S.H.I.T!, that I could've missed open doors, or I could've caused the doors to close. I'm thankful I had the wherewithal that despite the stinging pain of my tears, that I was able to keep my eyes on the prize. Many have gotten lost while Suffering Hardship and Internalizing Trauma, but I'm a living witness that you don't have to. You have the power to turn your negative S.H.I.T!, into positive SUCCESS!

Throughout the course of my life I questioned why it had to be so hard? Why did I have to fight to overcome the obstacles that were constantly set before me and today I know the answer to that question. When I made the decision, at a young age to never freeze up in the face of adversity, it helped me have a little resolve that I didn't know I had prior to that decision. I believe that was one of my first steps in owning my S.H.I.T! As I grew in age, I grew in practicing to own my S.H.I.T! With every piece of S.H.I.T! I encountered, I received needed practice to prepare me for recognizing, owning and getting through subsequent pieces of S.H.I.T! The character that me overcoming my S.H.I.T! has built has uniquely qualified me to stand in the gap for the least, last and lost. I no longer crumble easily. I'm able to withstand adversity when others falter. I've literally saved people's in very dangerous situations. I know lives can literally be saved by ordinary people because I witnessed that ordinary guy save that drowning child. If he could do it then so can I. I credit that experience with blessing me with the opportunity to save the lives of five precious individuals. One was a gunshot victim. The second was an SUV rollover victim who was ejected on the freeway. The third was a hit and run victim. The fourth was a victim who was passed out on a busy street. And the fifth and most notable save, for which I won a Hero Award, was Megan Kaplan. A teenager, whose car fell approximately 100 feet off a freeway interchange, caught fire and exploded seconds after myself and my son extricated her from her car. I ran 50 meters, with Megan in my arms, to safety. I definitely attribute my fearlessness to overcoming my S.H.I.T!

Just as I know that S.H.I.T! can put you in precarious situations, I also know that owning your S.H.I.T! can put you in victorious situations. When I look back over my S.H.I.T!, especially the S.H.I.T! with my mom, I realize that it was for my good. Going through it didn't feel good but now that I am older, and I see that it prepared me for the woman I am today. As ironic as it seems, I am who I am because of my mom. While I learned much of what not to do, as a parent, from my mom. I also learned from my grandmother that there was good in my mom, if I looked hard enough. Dear challenged me to find the good in my mom. So I took her up on her challenge. I looked long and hard and I realized that my mom taught me that in a room full of 100 people, I "better have the courage to do what is right even when the 99 others are doing wrong." That lesson about courage has carried me through many tough times. My mom taught me the value of education and how it can change your life and my life is definitely changed for the better, in large part, due to my education. My mom taught me that civil rights are worth dying for. Consequently I've been able to fight for people's civil rights. My mom taught me to help the less fortunate through our volunteering at the SHAPE Center food cooperative and I continue to find ways to volunteer to help humanity. My mom taught me the value of eating fresh fruits and vegetables and fight for access to fresh fruits and vegetables in historically disadvantaged neighborhoods. My mom taught me the value of keeping it moving like when our house burned down one night and we, the kids went to school, and my mom went to work the next day. I continue to keep it moving even in difficult times. The point I'm making is, in Owning My S.H.I.T, I had to accept that my mom is a big reason why I'm successful.

None of my successes would've ever manifested, had I chosen to stay STUCK in an impoverished mindset with pain as my crutch. Owning My S.H.I.T! took a lot of guts, and with a lot of odds stacked against me, but I MADE A CHOICE to LIVE and not DIE! I MADE A CHOICE to SEE THAT BETWEEN THOSE ODDS WERE SPACES THAT I COULD CREEP THROUGH TO MINIMIZE OR AVOID THE ODDS AGAINST ME!

Therefore, as I come to a close, no matter what you're facing at this very moment, YOU, yes YOU have the POWER to reshape your life, by first taking a long hard look in the mirror…Self-Analysis! Once you evaluate yourself, stop pointing fingers at everyone else for your inability to be where you think you should be, sift through your S.H.I.T!, take ownership of your contribution to your S.H.I.T!, and figure out how to throw it away, then and only then, will you be able to become your authentic self with the power to be who you were created to be. The fact that I had to live through and survive rape, murder, suicide, child sexual abuse, domestic violence, family dysfunction, poverty and other S.H.I.T! is a testament to my strong belief that owning your S.H.I.T! decreases the chances that your S.H.I.T! can be used against you effectively! Please be advised that to OWN YOUR S.H.I.T! IS TO BE

THE S.H.I.T!! if you work long enough and hard enough! With these words in mind, to use a track analogy: On your mark. Get set. Own Your S.H.I.T!

Memoir by
Coach Leroy Burrell

When I first met Jolanda Jones in 1985, my freshman year at the University of Houston, she was starting her Sophomore year after winning an NCAA championship in the Heptathlon, placing at the US Nationals in track and field, earning a position on the US World University Games Team, all while earning the highest GPA on the track team. She was the smartest, most talented, articulate and opinionated athlete I had ever met. As an incoming freshman I was in awe. I knew instantly that it would be best for me to get to know her because she appeared to have everything working for her.

As I got to know her better, I learned that she, like me had come from a difficult background, a broken home, was raised by a single mother and bounced from school to school. We had and continue to have a lot in common. I didn't know that she was a victim of abuse, nor about the death and loss she suffered, and the obstacles she had to overcome to get to her second year at UH. I could not have foreseen the additional difficulties she would face, and the ghosts from her past that would continue to haunt her future. True to form Jolanda, overcame them all.

Jolanda Jones was a Champion heptathlete in the sport of track and field back then and a multi-faceted, multi-talented champion in life doing the same in her law career, and as a staunch advocate for education and the disadvantaged in her community. This memoir is about leaping the pitfalls, jumping the barriers, throwing off the weights that hinder you and running the race of life, no matter the season, fearlessly. This is her story of clearing the pitfalls of life and overcoming her (and others) S.H.I.T!

Olympic Gold Medalist

Head Men's and Women's Track and Field Coach – UH
Houston, Texas

Memoir by
Coach Marti L. Burch
(aka: Coach Toulmin)

The first time I met Jolanda Jones was the in the Spring of her eighth-grade school year. As the track coach of Elsik High School, I always went to the middle schools to inspire the young athletes to stay involved in track and field during high school. Jolanda jumped at the chance to run AAU track in the summer and when she qualified for the Junior Olympics in Hattiesburg, Mississippi, I approached her mom with the option of taking her along with others who were running.

I don't really remember how she placed, but I do remember giving her her first pair of track shoes (spikes) which really thrilled her (even though they were boys' shoes because I didn't have any girl's shoes big enough to fit her). Just the fact that it was her first pair of spikes is what made her happy.

I don't think Jo's mom liked me very much and probably thought that I was just another "upidity" white woman taking advantage of Jo's talent. She was never very friendly, and I hope I'm wrong, but that was the way I felt every time we spoke. She did, however, trust me to take Jolanda under my wing and pick her up for 6:00 a.m. workouts along with others I took to school. I don't think I ever convinced Jo's mom that I truly cared for the well-being of all my athletes and I didn't (and still do not) see color.

Jolanda's talent was quite evident because she was so coachable and willing to try to do whatever she was asked to do to improve her performance whether it be running, jumping, or relays. Often, she would finish her work out and go back to run with those who were slower to encourage them to finish.

It was fun to watch Jolanda grow into the young lady/athlete/ leader she has become. As a freshman at Elsik, she would hang with the coaches on the bus rides and at track meets and take in all she could. By the time she was a junior, she was the leader and would express her points of view quite candidly.

Jolanda even ran cross country her junior year to support the team (or so I thought). She later informed me it was because of the shoes the cross country team got to wear. As it turned out, she was vital to the winning season. This caused a bit of a problem because she ended up beating her best friend, who was the fastest distance runner prior to Jo running cross country. All in all, I hope that they worked it out because the two of them were unstoppable until her friend came down with a foot injury.

Jolanda's senior year was her BEST high school year in track and field and I knew it would be. I predicted she could/would single handedly win the state team championship and she did. The boys' coach took her under his wing to help her accomplish that dream.

There's not much more I remember as it has been a while and I'm old; but as I recall, Jolanda took extra measures to "prove her point" on occasions and I would use her "technique" and turn it into a humorous strategy to get her to "lighten up". Jo was always so serious. I believe teenagers would call her "bossy" even though it was just her way of leadership.

Thinking back over this lifetime, I can say I wasn't surprised Jolanda was the first to be voted off of the hit TV show "Survivor Palau", during Season 10. I saw her "leadership" skills be used so early in the process. I remember saying to myself, "Back off, Jolanda, and don't come on too strong with these folks you just met." But in true Jolanda form, she went bursting right on through telling those people how it should be done and winning immunity. Jo's leadership and talent had a way of intimidating people who were insecure.

PS: It has been great to be back in touch with you, Jolanda, after all these years and to learn of the many accomplishments you've achieved throughout your young lifetime. Although we didn't always agree on everything, I believe we always had a mutual respect for each other. I am extremely proud of you and love you like the daughter I never had.

Marti L. Burch (aka: Coach Toulmin)
High School Track and Field Coach
Bedford, Texas

Memoir by
Cathy J. Lewis

I'm Jolanda's dad's youngest sister, Cathy. I'm the youngest of 12 kids and I'm only 7 years older than Jo. So, I've known Jolanda her whole life. I remember her as young as 2 year's old, being a performer and never tiring of being asked to dance, sing, spell etc... She was not shy. Family members would have her perform many nursery rhymes, but the one I remember most was "I'm a Little Teapot". She would do it with the same energy as she did the very first time, every time. Jo's mom taught her how to speak correctly by pronouncing and enunciating her words when she spoke. Gwen never talked baby talk to Jolanda nor did she allow anyone else to. I think the name of Jo's book is ironic because I thought it very impressive to have her tell my friends what she did when going to the bathroom. Without missing a beat, and on que, Jo would say "urinate, defecate or bowel movement". She was all of 2 year's old. At 2 she used those proper words and now she's using you know what. Gwen would've never allowed her to use that word when she was growing up. So, from a very young girl, she was owning it but she didn't realize it.

Jo was always very smart, I gave her $20 for A's, $10 for B's; Jo never brought home less than a B. One teacher gave Jo a poor grade because of her incessant questioning. Her mom showed up and got it corrected quickly. Our family always knew that Jo would be successful, because she worked hard at everything she did. No class could move forward if she didn't understand. Track and basketball were outlets for Jo. She was a true athlete. I remember someone stole her track shoes at the State Track meet, so she couldn't run and be disqualified. She ran in borrowed shoes and won anyway.

Jo's mom taught her to take care and keep up with her things. When she visited her grand parents' home, she didn't keep her things together. When Jo's mom arrived, everybody in the house was running around trying to get her things together. We were all afraid because Jo's mom was strict and played no games, even to this day. I think Jo got her strength from her mom, she was young, determined and strong.

Jo's book will share so many stories that will help you understand Jo. I'm her aunt. I know many but not all of her struggles, but I just knew, despite everything she endured, that she would figure out how to be successful. I think Jo's book will show the world how she overcame many of the curses that plagued our family like suicide, murder and prison. We could all see that Jo was going to be that one to beat the odds. At some point, most of our family and neighborhood were rooting for her. I think, after reading this book, you'll root for her too. I think a lot of people can learn from Jo about how to use tremendous adversity as a character and success-builder. She's an example of the notion that if you work long enough and hard enough and don't make excuses, that you will eventually succeed. I'm proud of Jo. Her success didn't come easy. It came with hard work and sacrifice and I'm finally glad to see her truly happy. She deserves it.

Cathy J. Lewis
Aunt
Houston, Texas

Author Bio

Jolanda "Jo" Jones

HISD Trustee, and former City Council Member and Warrior Lawyer for the People - Jolanda Jones - is both respected and influential across the United States but she didn't start out that way.

She started out as the oldest of five children (who was with her dad when he killed himself) of a single mom who struggled to keep a roof over their head, food on the table, electricity, gas and running water in whatever house or apartment she could pass a credit check on. Often, they went without. She is a survivor of horrific abuse and the suicide of her father, the murder of her brother, aunt and numerous cousins, among other tragedies.

Notwithstanding these obstacles, Jolanda is committed to helping the disenfranchised through her legal, social and political advocacy. Her personal journey is riveting and inspiring. Most people might be distracted from their life's purpose when they live the life Jolanda lived but not so for her. She instead has used her setbacks to motivate her to be fearless and empowering in the face of tremendous adversity. She is an unapologetic and unafraid warrior for those forgotten about and stepped on by society and is a tireless advocate for the human rights of all people.

She is a world-class athlete who won 4 national titles and earned a spot on multiple United States Track and Field Teams. She was an All-American in both basketball and track and field. She single-handedly won the Texas State UIL Team

Championship, by winning the 800m, 400m and High Jump, setting the state record of 6'1 ½", and getting second in the Long Jump. She was All-State in Cross Country.

She has won numerous awards for business, athletics, academics and public service, including numerous Halls of Fame. She is also a great mom who raised her son, Jiovanni, to be on the Dean's List, a college graduate, social justice advocate, and now, law student, just like her.

Her passion is reforming the criminal justice system, eradicating gun violence, stopping domestic violence, reforming the political system and educating people on their rights, through her lecture series, including "Know Your Rights With The Police," which she has given since 1999, and "Surviving Domestic Abuse." Jolanda also represents various survivors of mass shootings, including some from Parkland and Santa Fe.

She was the star of the WEtv show "Sisters in Law," where she unwaveringly fought for her clients, and she was a castaway, on Season 10, of CBS Survivor Palau.

"Owning My S.H.I.T!" is Jolanda's second book, the first being the "Scholathlete's Survival Guide: Essential Study Skills for the Scholar Athlete", where she is the co-author, which is also available on Amazon. This labor of love that is "Owning My S.H.I.T! is a direct response to public demand from her over 20 years of motivational speaking across the United States.

Contact for Speaking Engagements:
Email: owningmyS.H.I.T!book@gmail.com
Website 1: http://owningmyS.H.I.T!.com
Website 2: JolandaJonesConsulting.com
Facebook: @JolandaJoJones
Instagram: @JolandaJones
Twitter: @JonesJolanda

About the Cover

I know that both the cover and title are provocative. I intended it that way. In my mind, it was the only cover that encapsulated my authentic self. I'd dreamt and visualized the cover before any photo was taken. While it was still a thought, I shared my vision, of the cover, with a few friends. Some warned me about using the word S.H.I.T! They opined that it was an ugly word. A curse word. A harsh word. I respectfully disagreed with their characterization. They suggested that I use the word "obstacle" or "challenge" instead, or something to that effect. In their minds, those words were nicer. The hardships and trauma I survived were more than merely obstacles or challenges. As I struggled to get through them, there was nothing nice or palatable about them. No word was more appropriate than the word S.H.I.T! The struggles were ugly. They were dirty. And, they stank to high hell. So why would I put lipstick on a pig when it's still a pig?

Apart from that, S.H.I.T! is an acronym for Suffering Hardship Internalizing Trauma, which is exactly why I had such a difficult life. I didn't understand how not to internalize my hardship and trauma and that crucial lack of understanding contributed to many of my difficult situations and bad decisions. For me, accepting truth, regardless of the ugliness of it, was essential to me successfully overcoming my S.H.I.T! If I softened or mitigated the ugliness, then I wasn't fully prepared to defeat my demons. So regardless of my friends' trepidation about the word S.H.I.T!, I made an executive decision that it was my book, my life and that the word that best described what held me back was S.H.I.T! So, S.H.I.T! it was.

The oufit. The bustier. The shorts. The tulle peacock skirt. The stilettos. The long silk gloves. The minimal jewelry. The all black. The power red. The red chair. The pile of shit on the red tray. The aroma rising from the shit. Me holding the pile of shit. That's all me. I'm eclectic. I'm bold. I'm daring. I'm strong. I'm sexy. I'm a mom. I'm smart. I work hard. I'm an athlete. I'm unafraid. I work out. I'm confident. I'm blonde by choice. I'm short-haired by choice. I'm professional. I'm educated. I'm a woman who's not afraid of men. I believe strong bodies make strong minds. I'm ambitious. I'm aggressive. I'm patient. I'm loved. I'm hated. I'm feared. I'm intimidating. I'm funny. I'm serious. I'm caring. I'm your best friend. I'm your worst nightmare. I go after what I want like a heat seeking missile. I'm unapologetic. I'm raw. I'm polarizing. The people that love me are willing to die for me.

The people that hate me would kill me if they thought they could get away with it. To many, I'm an oxymoron. Me standing in that outfit with my foot on that red chair holding my own S.H.I.T!, for you all to see, is me telling you that this is my S.H.I.T! I own it! You can't use it against me because I will not allow you to! I'm not afraid of my S.H.I.T! I'm putting it in your face and saying to you, now what? It's symbolic of the boldness with which I face myself and the world and dare you to say something. The cover is totally contradictory of how I dealt with myself and my life before I learned to own my S.H.I.T! I wanted to equate the visual picture of shit with my S.H.I.T! ~ like suicide, murder, rape, domestic violence and so forth and so on. The juxtaposition of beauty with ugliness is the point. You can be all of those things and still be okay.

I've learned that I can't please everyone, so if you don't like me or the cover then that's not my problem, it's yours. Self-love and appreciation is essential to overcoming S.H.I.T! Your love and appreciation for yourself will definitely sustain you when others won't or don't. So, here's to you figuring out who you are and creating the cover of your life whether people understand it or not. All that matters is that you are true to yourself. That is what this cover is all about. Cheers!

www.ingramcontent.com/pod-product-compliance
Lightning Source LLC
Chambersburg PA
CBHW070640150426
42811CB00050B/443